EXTEND
education

ReviseIB

Global politics

TestPrep: DP Exam Practice Workbook

C000152646

A note from us

While every effort has been made to provide accurate advice on the assessments for this subject, the only authoritative and definitive source of guidance and information is published in the official subject guide, teacher support materials, specimen papers and associated content published by the IB. Please refer to these documents in the first instance for advice and guidance on your assessments.

Any exam-style questions in this book have been written to help you practise and revise your knowledge and understanding of the content before your exam. Remember that the actual exam questions may not look like this.

Christopher McQuillan and Stephen Rudall

SL & HL
Standard Level & Higher Level

Published by Extend Education Ltd., Alma House, 73 Rodney Road, Cheltenham, United Kingdom, GL50 1HT

www.extendeducation.com

The right of Christopher McQuillan and Stephen Rudall to be identified as authors of this work has been asserted by them with the Copyright, Designs and Patents Act 1988.

Reviewed by Brian Hull

Typesetting by York Publishing Solutions Pvt. Ltd., INDIA

Cover photo by Anthony Delanoix on Unsplash

First published 2020

24 23 22 21 20

10 9 8 7 6 5 4 3 2 1

ISBN 978-1-913121-05-1

Author acknowledgements

Christopher McQuillan: I would like to thank my girlfriend for bringing me cups of tea. Stephen Rudall: Thanks to my wife for her infinite patience and my parents for sparking my interest in the world around me from a young age.

Other important information

A reminder that Extend Education is not in any way affiliated with the International Baccalaureate.

Many people have worked to create this book. We go through rigorous editorial processes, including separate answers checks and expert reviews of all content. However, we all make mistakes. So if you notice an error in the paper, please let us know at info@extendeducation.co.uk so we can make sure it is corrected at the earliest possible opportunity.

If you are an educator with a passion for creating content and would like to write for us, please contact info@extendeducation.co.uk or write to us through the contact form on our website www.extendeducation.co.uk.

CONTENTS

You can find an extra, free Paper 1 to practise here!

HOW TO USE THIS BOOK   4

EXPLAIN

KNOWING YOUR PAPER   5

SHOW

SHOWING WHAT YOU KNOW   12

TEST

TESTING WHAT YOU KNOW   23

SET A

Paper 1   23
Paper 2   28

SET B

Paper 1   44
Paper 2   48

SET C

Paper 1   64
Paper 2   68

ANSWERS   84

Set A: Paper 1   84
      Paper 2   84

Set B: Paper 1   87
      Paper 2   87

Set C: Paper 1   90
      Paper 2   90

Permissions
Hong Kong protests, photo by Joseph Chan on Unsplash (p.12); Kuyper, J. W., Linnér, B. and Schroeder, H. (2018), 'Non-state actors in hybrid global climate governance: justice, legitimacy, and effectiveness in a post-Paris era', WIREs Climate Change, Volume 9, Issue 1, e497 doi:10.1002/wcc.497, Attribution 4.0 International (CC BY 4.0) (p.13); United Nations, Charter of the United Nations, 24 October 1945, 1 UNTS XVI, available at: www.refworld.org/docid/3ae6b3930.html (p.13); Roccia, G. (2012), Do IGOs Decrease thePossibility of Conflict. E-IT.INFO [online]. Retrieved from: www.e-ir.info/2012/01/03/do-igos-decrease-the-possibility-of-conflict/ (p.13); Feenstra, Robert C., Inklaar, R. and Timmer, M. T. (2015), "The Next Generation of the Penn World Table" American Economic Review, Volume 105, Issue 10, pp. 3150–3182. Available for download at: www.ggdc.net/pwt (p.23); Adapted from an article published on the BBC: Ruggeri, A (2018), How can you measure what makes a country great [online]. Retrieved from: http://www.bbc.com/future/story/20180111-how-can-you-measure-what-makes-a-country-great [Accessed on: 06 November 2019] (p.24); Adapted from a lecture by Professor Williamson in the series 'Practitioners of Development', delivered at the World Bank on January 13, 2004. (Full speech is available at; www.piie.com/publications/papers/williamson0204.pdf) (p.24); Wooldridge, A (2012), "Special Report: State Capitalism", The Economist (p.25); CIA Factbook (2016) (p.44); Adapted from a blog article: Hussain, Z. (2014), "Can political stability hurt economic growth?", World Bank Blogs. [online]. Retrieved from: blogs.worldbank.org/endpovertyinsouthasia/can-political-stability-hurt-economic-growth (p.45); Economic and Social Council (2019), Report of the UN Committee for Development Policy [online]. Supplement: 13. Retrieved from: undocs.org/en/E/2019/33] (p.45); OECD (2019), Why Open Markets Matter [online]. Retrieved from: www.oecd.org/trade/understanding-the-global-trading-system/why-open-markets-matter/ (p.46); Donnelly, J (2017), Human Rights, in: Bayliss, J, et al., The Globalization of World Politics, 7th Ed. Oxford: Oxford University Press, p. 500 (p.64); Regilme, S. S. F. (2019), "The Global Politics of Human Rights: From Human Rights to Human Dignity?", International Political Science Review, Volume 40, Issue 2, pp. 279–290(p.65); Rathgeber, T (2014), "Documentation: International Legal Human Rights Framework: Human Rights and the Institutionalisation of ASEAN: An Ambiguous Relationship", Journal of Current Southeast Asian Affairs, Volume 33, Issue 3, pp. 131–165(p.65)

HOW TO USE THIS BOOK

This excellent exam practice book has been designed to help you prepare for your global politics exam. It is divided into three sections.

EXPLAIN

The EXPLAIN section gives you a rundown of your paper, including the number of marks available, how much time you'll have and the assessment objectives (AOs) and command terms. There's also a handy checklist of the topics that you can use as a revision checklist.

SHOW

The SHOW section gives you some examples of different questions you will come across in the exam. It's designed to help you learn the question types and the kinds of answers you can give to get the maximum number of marks.

TEST

This is your chance to try out what you've learned. The TEST section has full sets of exam-style practice papers filled with the same type and number of questions that you can expect to see in the exam. The first set of papers has a lot of helpful tips and suggestions for answering the questions. The middle set has more general advice – make sure you have revised before testing yourself with this set. The last set gives no help at all. Not one single hint! Make sure you do this one a bit closer to your exam to check what else you might need to revise.

Set A

Paper 1 (SL&HL) & Paper 2 (SL&HL)

Presented with a lot of tips and guidance to help you to get to the correct answer and boost your confidence!

Use these papers early on in your revision.

Set B

Paper 1 (SL&HL) & Paper 2 (SL&HL)

Presented with fewer helpful suggestions so you have to rely on your revision to answer these.

Test yourself using these papers when you're a bit more confident.

Set C

Paper 1 (SL&HL) & Paper 2 (SL&HL)

Presented with space to add your own notes and no guidance – the perfect way to test you are exam ready.

Use these papers as close as you can to the exam.

All questions are presented with **ANSWERS** so you can check how you did in your practice papers.

Because of the different question options in Paper 2, you can test yourself multiple times in Set A , B and C!

Take a look at some of the helpful features in these books that are designed to support you as you do your practice papers.

These will point you in the direction of the right answer!

Beware of making the common and easy-to-avoid mistakes!

These are referred to as AOs all the way through this book

These are general hints for answering the questions.

These flag up common or easy-to-make mistakes that might cost you marks.

This box reminds you of the Assessment Objective being tested.

ANSWER ANALYSIS

These boxes include advice on how to get the most possible marks for your answer.

COMMAND TERMS

These boxes outline what the command term is asking you to do.

The command terms are like a clue to how you should answer your questions.

These show you when the questions have other interdisciplinary links.

Like to TOK or Extended Essay!

KNOWING YOUR PAPER

Understanding exactly what skills and what knowledge will be tested in your global politics exams is critical to getting high marks. The skills and knowledge taught in the whole global politics course will be tested in two papers: Paper 1 and Paper 2. Each question on each paper is approached in a different way. This section will help make sure there are no surprises! The table below is a bit dry but it's important to learn how the exam paper is structured, how much time to spend on each section and how many questions to answer.

> Managing your time is key. Make sure to practise writing your answers in timed conditions, allocating more or less time to each question depending on the marks available.

How are you assessed?

Whether you are taking Standard Level or Higher Level, you will sit **two** written papers for your exam.

	Standard Level	Higher Level
Paper 1	Four short-answer questions that use the source stimulus material provided. The questions link to **only one** of the four units of study. Four sources are used and they must be integrated into your answers. **All questions are compulsory.**	
	Answer four questions	Answer four questions
	30% of entire grade	20% of entire grade
	25 marks	25 marks
	1 hour and 15 minutes	1 hour and 15 minutes

> Paper 1 timings per question:
> - Q1: 9 mins
> - Q2: 12 mins
> - Q3: 24 mins
> - Q4: 30 mins

	Standard Level	Higher Level
Paper 2	Essay-style responses covering **all four** units of study, with no source stimulus material. Two essays per unit of study are provided (eight essays in total); however, **only one essay per unit** can be chosen. Each question is worth 25 marks and the question stems indicate how to approach the essay structure.	
	Answer two questions	Answer three questions
	45% of entire grade	40% of entire grade
	50 marks	75 marks
	1 hour and 45 minutes	2 hours and 45 minutes

> **SL** Paper 2 approximate timings (with a bit left over for extra checks and preparation time)
> - Q1: 50 mins
> - Q2: 50 mins

> **HL** Paper 2 approximate timings (with a bit left over for extra checks and preparation time):
> - Q1: 50 mins
> - Q2: 50 mins
> - Q3: 50 mins

Your assessment objectives

Assessment objective	Which questions test this?	Example questions
AO1: KNOWLEDGE AND UNDERSTANDING Can you demonstrate key political concepts? How about contemporary issues? Is your source material relevant? Can you talk about political issues in the right context? HL students, can you also show in-depth understanding of two detailed case studies?	Paper 1, Question 1 Paper 2, Questions 1–8	**Question 1**: With reference to Source A, identify **three** different measurements of development. **[3 marks]** **Questions 1–8:** Examine the claim that power in global politics is quantifiable to military power. **[25 marks]**

> AO1 command terms: describe, outline, define, identify

Assessment objective	Which questions test this?	Example questions
AO2: APPLICATION AND ANALYSIS Can you analyse contemporary political issues in different contexts? Can you think of relevant examples? You'll need to do this in order to create and make an argument. And you'll also need to use your knowledge to analyse and inform experiential learning about a political issue. HL students, can you also analyse political issues in two case studies?	Paper 1, Question 2 Paper 2, Questions 1–8	**Question 1**: Using Source C and **one** example you have studied, explain the reasons why there may be some disagreement on focus upon GDP or GNP by mainstream models of development. **[4 marks]** **Questions 1–8:** To what extent has the concept of state sovereignty evolved in the 21st century? **[25 marks]**
AO3: SYNTHESIS AND EVALUATION In this AO, your ability to evaluate your own knowledge and evidence from sources is tested. Can you compare and contrast, synthesize and evaluate different perspectives and talk about different beliefs, biases and prejudices and where these come from? Can you also synthesize and evaluate the results of experiential learning and theoretical perspectives on a political issue? HL students, can you also synthesize and evaluate different approaches to and interpretations of political issues in two case studies?	Paper 1, Question 3 Paper 1, Question 4 Paper 2, Questions 1–8	**Questions 3:** Contrast what Source B **and** D reveal about development. **[8 marks]** **Question 4**: Using the sources **and** your own knowledge, evaluate to what extent non-state actors influence state sovereignty. **[10 marks]** **Questions 1–8:** Discuss the view that without political stability sustained development cannot be achieved. **[25 marks]**
AO4: USE AND APPLICATION OF APPROPRIATE SKILLS Can you produce well-structured written material that uses the appropriate terms? Is your answer clearly and logically organized? Can you demonstrate evidence of research, excellent organization and referencing? HL students, you must also be able to clearly present ideas orally.	Paper 1, Question 3 Paper 1, Question 4 Paper 2, Questions 1–8	**Questions 3:** Compare and contrast what Source C **and** Source D reveal about the role of IGOs in global politics. **[8 marks]** **Question 4**: 'Mainstream interpretations of development are nothing more than the exploitation of peripheral states by core states.' With reference to Sources A to D **and** your own knowledge, to what extent do you agree with this claim? **[10 marks]** **Questions 1–8:** Examine the claim that positive peace is unobtainable. **[25 marks]**

AO2 command terms: analyse, express, explain, distinguish

AO3 command terms: contrast, compare, compare and contrast, discuss, evaluate, examine, justify, to what extent

AO4 command terms: examine, evaluate, discuss

Before you begin your exam

You could be tested on any of the four units of study, so you must revise and be comfortable answering questions on all of them. The core units are:

(1) Power, sovereignty and international relations

(2) Human rights

(3) Development

(4) Peace and conflict.

Check that you understand each term by writing a brief definition for it below. Tick the box when you have revised enough to confidently answer a question on the concept.

	Key concept	Definition	Revised
Power, sovereignty and international relations	Power		☐
	Sovereignty		☐
	Legitimacy		☐
	Interdependence		☐
Human rights	Human rights		☐
	Justice		☐
	Liberty		☐
	Equality		☐
Development	Development		☐
	Globalization		☐
	Inequality		☐
	Sustainability		☐

For Paper 1 (SL & HL), questions will focus on **one** of your four units of study.

SL For Paper 2 (SL) you must write **two** essays covering **two** different units of study.

HL For Paper 2 (HL) you must write **three** essays covering **three** different units of study.

	Key concept	Definition	Revised
Peace and conflict	Peace		☐
	Conflict		☐
	Violence		☐
	Non-violence		☐

An important part of your global politics course is the ability to study political issues at different levels. The six levels are: global, international, regional, national, local and community. Using the table below, make sure you understand the different levels of analysis by adding in a brief description, one or two examples and ticking the box when you feel confident enough to use your knowledge in the exam.

Level of analysis	Definition	Revised
Global		☐
International		☐
Regional		☐
National		☐
Local		☐
Community		☐

An example of a global event could be climate change.

Not only will a global issue have many local implications, but a local issue will also affect other levels of analysis.

To decide the appropriate level of analysis you should look at what is at stake and what the question is asking you to do.

Case studies

In global politics it is important that you include case studies from the real world in your answers. These should be as up to date and relevant as possible (yes, you can use an event from last week if relevant).

The case studies should have happened within your lifetime (the 'lifetime' rule). You should only use case studies from outside of your lifetime when using them as simple context, for example when discussing key vocabulary. **Examples from outside of your lifetime will not be viewed as case studies, meaning you will not be given credit for them in your exam**.

You need to include relevant and explained case studies in your answer to gain high marks. Alongside the sixteen key terms, six levels of analysis and key course content, the quality of your written answers will rely on your knowledge of case studies.

Two different methods are often used when including case studies in your answers. These are the 'breadth' and 'depth' approaches.

Breadth

This approach attempts to use as many case study examples as possible in the exam, taking examples from different regions and different levels of analysis to evidence the arguments.

Depth

This approach uses a more limited number of case studies. However, it applies a more detailed knowledge of the examples as evidence within the response.

Neither technique is correct or better than the other; they are simply different styles of writing.

Make a note in the table below of the case studies you plan to use in the exam.

Power, sovereignty and international relations	1. 2. 3. 4.
Human rights	1. 2. 3. 4.
Development	1. 2. 3. 4.
Peace and conflict	1. 2. 3. 4.

Paper 2: When writing a 25-mark response, you should develop **at least one** case study example per argument for a depth-style case study usage. For a breadth-style approach, you should have two case study examples developed per argument.

Paper 2: Develop in detail the case studies which most readily apply to each question.

The genocide of the Rohingya is a case study that could be used in the human rights unit.

You could download a news app as a way of keeping up to date with current affairs.

It is not enough to only be aware of what happens in a case study. You need to understand the different analysis levels (for example, international or local) and perspectives (for example, gender or class) within it.

For TOK, you might consider the problems of using case studies as a way of acquiring knowledge.

A new argument should start a new paragraph.

What to do in your Paper 1 exam

Identify the unit being examined.

Read the first exam question. Highlight command words and key terms.

Write any additional information you might need next to relevant questions. Briefly plan the exam response.

Read the source being examined. Highlight any key terms asked for in the question. Highlight any quotes you wish to use.

Write the exam response in the amount of time you have allocated for that question.

Move on to the next question and repeat the previous steps.

What to do in your Paper 2 exam

Select the unit you are most confident in.

Read both exam questions.

Highlight the command words and key terms. Make sure you understand what each question is asking you to do.

Decide which of the two questions you are more confident in writing.

Quickly note down as much course information as you can into each of the arguments (paragraphs), including the case studies you will use.

Create a basic plan of your response to both questions, with the different arguments (paragraphs) outlined.

Write the exam response to the plan you are more confident in writing.

Move on to the unit you are second most confident with, and repeat the previous steps.

HL only: Choose one last unit and repeat the previous steps.

How to get high marks

When taking your exams you need to demonstrate your abilities in the following.

Knowledge and understanding

Firstly, you must use your written responses to show thorough knowledge and understanding of the four course units. You need to show not just that you are aware of the key course content, but also that you fully understand the different requirements of each question.

Key theories and case studies

Secondly, you must display the ability to integrate key theories related to the course with case study examples from the real world. This can be applied in all of the questions throughout both your papers.

Academic structure

Finally, your answers need good academic structure. You need to answer the questions the way the IB requires and as explained in this workbook. There are different requirements for each question type that you need to fulfil in order to get high marks.

Use your notes to condense all of the key vocabulary, knowledge and theories, making it easier to revise.

During your revision, create a bank of case studies that apply to each unit of study and each topic within a unit. These do not need to be exclusive: a case study can be used more than once in an exam. However, you must clearly explain how it relates to the specific argument under discussion.

If you follow the Paper 1 structure when answering Paper 2 then you will not meet the full IB requirements for Paper 2 responses and so will not receive the highest marks.

SHOWING WHAT YOU KNOW

In this section, some model answers have been shown to give you an idea of what you could write in the exam. These are not the only possible answers, but should help you to identify a good approach when sitting your exam. There is also an explanation of why they are good examples, along with some tips, advice and common mistakes you should be mindful of when answering a question.

Paper 1

For Paper 1, you will be given four unseen sources to study. These sources will be followed by four questions. You must answer all of the questions, using the sources in your responses. We have given you an example of a full-mark answer for each question below, so you can get familiar with the question types and how to best approach them.

Unit 1: Power, sovereignty and international relations

Read all the sources carefully and answer all the questions that follow.

Source A

Hong Kong Protests

> You will be allowed five minutes of reading time at the beginning of this exam where you are not allowed to write or highlight!

Source B

Non-state actors are formally and informally woven into the Paris Agreement performing a range of different and increasingly important functions. Non-state actors will act as watchdogs of the NDCs (*nationally determined contributions*) enhancing transparency, facilitating the stocktakes, and pressuring for the ratcheting up of NDCs every 5 years. Likewise, non-state actors will act as contributors and governing partners through orchestration as they are encouraged by the Agreement 'to scale up their climate actions'.

[Source: Kuyper, J. W., Linnér, B. and Schroeder, H. (2018), 'Non-state actors in hybrid global climate governance: justice, legitimacy, and effectiveness in a post-Paris era', WIREs Climate Change, Volume 9, Issue 1, e497. doi:10.1002/wcc.497, Attribution 4.0 International (CC BY 4.0)]

NON-STATE ACTOR
Someone with political influence who isn't linked to a particular country.

STOCKTAKES
Counting up the number of contributions.

RATCHETING UP
Increasing the amount of something.

ORCHESTRATION
Planning and coordination.

Source C

Article 1

The Purposes of the United Nations are:

1. To maintain international peace and security, and to that end: to take effective collective measures for the prevention and removal of threats to the peace, and for the suppression of acts of aggression or other breaches of the peace, and to bring about by peaceful means, and in conformity with the principles of justice and international law, adjustment or settlement of international disputes or situations which might lead to a breach of the peace.

2. To develop friendly relations among nations based on respect for the principle of equal rights and self-determination of peoples, and to take other appropriate measures to strengthen universal peace.

3. To achieve international co-operation in solving international problems of an economic, social, cultural, or humanitarian character, and in promoting and encouraging respect for human rights and for fundamental freedoms for all without distinction as to race, sex, language, or religion.

4. To be a centre for harmonizing the actions of nations in the attainment of these common ends.

[Source: United Nations, Charter of the United Nations, 24 October 1945, 1 UNTS XVI, available at: https://www.refworld.org/docid/3ae6b3930.html]

SUPPRESSION
Actively stopping or reducing.

BREACHES
Disturbances that break an agreement or a law.

CONFORMITY
Following laws and sticking to agreements.

Source D

IGOs might be relevant in spreading common norms, but they still do not promote interstate peace because they need to have a complex, all-encompassing, institutional structure in order to actually limit conflict. They also need to be able to promulgate information to all members. Furthermore, IGOs that do not include in their agenda security issues, but only, for example, economic or cultural ones, will never be able to pursue peaceful management of conflict. Finally, if an IGO is only a group of different super-powers, then it will be difficult to find an agreement, because they will never give up their own individual interests (C. Boehmer, E. Gartzke, T. Nordstrom, 2004: 29).

[Source: Roccia, G. (2012), Do IGOs Decrease the Possibility of Conflict. E-IT.INFO [online]. Retrieved from: https://www.e-ir.info/2012/01/03/do-igos-decrease-the-possibility-of-conflict/]

INSTITUTIONAL
Organized, conventional and formal.

PROMULGATE
To promote and make something well-known.

1. Using Source A, identify **three** ways in which resistance movements can influence global politics. [3]

   - Resistance movements can provide resistance to legislation or state policies as evidenced via the public protests taking place in Source A from Hong Kong. These protests can use both violent and non-violent methods.

   - Resistance groups can act as a method of engagement in global politics for those who may have otherwise been apathetic, evidenced in the source with limited people actually protesting whilst a large quantity of the general public go about their daily lives. This is because members of resistance groups are often outside of the mainstream of political opinion within their states.

   - Resistance movements are often able to raise publicity globally for their cause, as seen with the media interest in this protest in Hong Kong and the images taken. This heightens public awareness and can act as an educational tool for the resistance movement.

2. With explicit reference to Source B and to **one** example you have studied, explain the effect non-state actors can have upon states. [4]

   One effect that non-state actors can have upon states is in bringing pressure to ensure state compliance with international agreements. As Source B specifically outlines, 'Non-state actors will act as watchdogs of the NDCs (nationally determined contributions) enhancing transparency'. This means that non-state actors, largely in this case referring to NGOs, affect states by exerting pressure to maintain transparency in their actions towards achieving the aims set down in international agreements. For example, in the UK, NGOs such as Greenpeace and the WWF-UK will be engaged in monitoring the activities of greenhouse gas emissions nationally, reporting and then making this data public. This will bring pressure to bear on the UK as an individual signatory state. Globally, groups such as Climate Action Tracker provide scientific data, which can be utilized at a national level.

   A second effect that non-state actors can have on states is outlined in Source B as 'non-state actors will act as contributors and governing partners'. This means that as non-state actors are often niche operators in specific fields, states will seek their advice and expert testimony when drafting new legislation or dealing with issues within their remit. For example, when drafting new legislation in

DESCRIBE, OUTLINE, IDENTIFY, DEFINE

Draw the AO1 knowledge directly from the source.

Source A can be textual, pictorial or data based. Make sure you know how to approach each type.

Your question 1 response should be in bullet point form – with three points separated out.

! Question 1 is specific. If it asks for three ways, give three ways. Do not over- or under-answer the question.

ANSWER ANALYSIS

Source A has been directly referenced. This answer would be worth the full 3 marks.

SUGGEST, DISTINGUISH, ANALYSE AND EXPLAIN

These terms mean you need to develop a concept so you can display a good understanding of it.

ANSWER ANALYSIS

Question 2 often begins 'With specific reference to Source B'. Do not write a response which does not make use of the named source.

Ethiopia regarding the operation of NGOs in summer 2019, Human Rights Watch offered their services to the Ethiopian government to ensure that the new legislation took account of previous problems regarding freedom of assembly for NGO members, amongst other issues. This shows a non-state actor affecting the policies implemented by the Ethiopian State.

Question 2 answers should be about two paragraphs long.

ANSWER ANALYSIS

This answer would be worth the full 4 marks.

3. Compare and contrast what Source C **and** Source D reveal about the role of intergovernmental organizations (IGOs) in global politics. [8]

Both source C and D place IGOs as prime actors in building international co-operation. Source C from the UN Charter specifically states that IGOs should be involved in 'international co-operation in solving international problems' and source D recognizes that some IGOs can be 'a group of different super-powers'. These statements evidence the important role given to IGOs within global politics by both sources. The role of the UN in conflict resolution in Sierra Leone, the African Union peacekeeping forces, or the IMF and World Bank enforcement of trade policies all give evidence of the role of IGOs in the international arena. These actions correlate with the neo-liberal school of thought and the deepening inter-relationships driven by IGOs.

However, by contrast, both sources disagree about the potential effectiveness of certain roles. Source C infers that IGOs will have great effectiveness in the global political arena, stating that they will 'take effective collective measures for the prevention and removal of threats to the peace, and for the suppression of acts of aggression or other breaches of the peace'. This contrasts with the perspective articulated in Source D, which argues that 'if an IGO is only a group of different super-powers, then it will be difficult to find an agreement, because they will never give up their own individual interests'. Therefore, clearly, there is a difference in perspective regarding the role of IGOs. Effective military action taken by NATO in North Africa in 2011 exemplifies the peacekeeping role of an IGO in international society. However, failure to act in the Syria civil conflict due to disagreement at the UN between the US/UK and Russia is evidence supporting the argument of Source D. Realist theorists such as Mearshimer would use these actions to display the primacy of the state, rather than the IGO, as the most important global actor, displaying the IGO's limited role in the international arena.

COMPARE AND CONTRAST

Questions with these terms want you to outline both similarities and differences. Compare means 'the same' and contrast means 'different'. You will need two similarities and two differences to answer this question.

ANSWER ANALYSIS

Using the word 'comparison' establishes the skill set this student is using.

ANSWER ANALYSIS

A similarity is outlined and established with direct quotations from both sources.

ANSWER ANALYSIS

A difference is outlined and established with direct quotations from both sources.

ANSWER ANALYSIS

Further evidence and knowledge, including relevant case studies, have been used to strengthen the argument.

A further comparison is visible when Source C argues that IGOs are responsible for 'promoting and encouraging respect for human rights and for fundamental freedoms for all without distinction as to race, sex, language, or religion'. To simplify, IGOs are responsible for spreading 'norms'. Source D fully agrees with this role as it argues that 'IGOs might be relevant in spreading common norms'. International agreements such as the Paris Climate Accords were negotiated via the UN as an IGO, creating a new set of international norms for carbon emission standards. Indeed, other IGO-negotiated treaties and conventions, such as the UDHR or UNCRC etc., have created a global legal framework for rights, evidencing their role establishing 'norms'.

However, as evidenced by the 2017 USA withdrawal from the Paris Climate Accords of 2015, member states are ultimately the signatories to these 'norms' and can remove the state if they choose, once again correlating with the Realist school of thought. The contrast in perspective regarding the role of IGOs between what Source C believes is possible and Source D believes to be achievable is evidenced in the quotes that IGOs are 'To be a centre for harmonizing the actions of nations in the attainment of these common ends' and 'IGOs that do not include in their agenda security issues, but only, for example, economic or cultural ones, will never be able to pursue peaceful management of conflict'.

4. Evaluate the claim that non-state actors challenge state sovereignty. Use all the sources **and** your own knowledge. **[10]**

Non-state actors are able to challenge or enhance state sovereignty in a number of clearly distinctive ways. Firstly, IGOs as non-state actors enhance state sovereignty due to the inherent need to be a state prior to joining. Therefore, IGOs as non-state actors give primacy to states, a fact recognized in both sources C and D. The UN Charter as laid out in Source C articulates the role of states in international society via IGOs, not other forms of non-state actors, placing them therefore at the heart of the international community above all others. This assertion of the importance of the state equates to a strengthening of state sovereignty by non-state actors. When the UN was originally founded it held 50 members in 1945; it is now composed of 195. Indeed, all fledgling states seek UN acceptance as a member, which is perceived to make them more legitimate. Recent examples

ANSWER ANALYSIS

Key concepts are embedded in the response. There is clear knowledge of interdependence.

COMPARE AND CONTRAST

Pay attention to the command terms – not all questions are both compare **and** contrast. Some only ask you to compare, others only ask you to contrast.

ANSWER ANALYSIS

This answer would be worth the full 8 marks.

EVALUATE

This means you need to make a judgement after presenting an argument which considers different perspectives. These can include theoretical perspectives or those from different societal or state actors. The term 'different perspectives' in the markband does not necessarily imply a 'two-sided' argument.

ANSWER ANALYSIS

Question 4 requires a deeper development of your own knowledge of the course, key concepts and case studies.

include the admittance of South Sudan in 2011, the most recently created fully sovereign state. If the UN does not grant full recognition and a member seat, such as has happened with Kosovo since 2008, the non-state actor can challenge the breakaway state's sought-after sovereignty.

Secondly, NGOs and non-state actors in civil society can help enhance state sovereignty by increasing a state's legitimacy if they are included in the democratic process. As outlined in Source B, non-state actors can have increasingly important roles with policy implementation and oversight, as 'non-state actors will act as contributors and governing partners'. By including their niche specialism and expertise in legislation and dispute resolution, state sovereignty is often increased as the state's legitimacy is increased. For example, during the drafting of workplace reform legislation, the ITUC and ILO will often advise local trade union actors on globally progressive workplace changes. Indeed, in trade-union-dense populations, such as Sweden (66%), Denmark (67%) and Finland (65%) (trade union membership in 2018), you will often find the most 'progressive' and 'gender neutral' working practices, but also three of the four happiest workforces on earth according to the Global Workforce Happiness Index, 2016. Therefore, we can see a positive impact upon governmental legitimacy and – by extension – state sovereignty in Scandinavia, due to worker contentment. This is driven by inclusion of trade unions as non-state actors in the political and legislative process.

Thirdly, non-state actors can weaken state sovereignty as their inability to act in times of security-based crisis can severely weaken state sovereignty. This is evidenced by the lack of military intervention by the UN to prevent the escalation of the Syrian Civil War from 2011 to date. As there are two opposing major powers on the UN Security Council with vetoes (USA and Russia), the organization has been paralysed by inaction in a conflict which has cost hundreds of thousands of civilian lives and also allowed the near collapse of two states, both Syria and Iraq, to the terrorist organization ISIL. This example clearly corroborates the author's comment in Source D 'if an IGO is only a group of different super-powers, then it will be difficult to find an agreement, because they will never give up their own individual interests'. Other examples of inaction

ANSWER ANALYSIS

This answer shows good knowledge of the basis of UN and modern issues in the development of state sovereignty.

ANSWER ANALYSIS

Evidence and the case study used is recent and relevant.

ANSWER ANALYSIS

Crossover of knowledge from other units displays an ability to synthesize and analyse relevant materials (HPI from development unit).

ANSWER ANALYSIS

Vocabulary used is appropriate and relevant – particularly the terms 'failed or failing state'.

ANSWER ANALYSIS

Question 4 requires a basic conclusion summarizing the basic arguments and answering the question set.

ANSWER ANALYSIS

All four sources have been used in this response, plus the student's own knowledge.

in Sierra Leone, Chad, Niger and Somalia have led to failed or failing states, challenging the state sovereignty and legitimacy.

Finally, state sovereignty can also be weakened by non-state actors when they express dissatisfaction with the current regime, often displaying a rejection of that state's sovereignty over a minority group, or a rejection of policies related to particular groups. Source A clearly articulates certain residents of Hong Kong rejecting the actions taken by the mainland government. An interpretation of Source B can be made that the non-state actors are being included in the process so as to avoid civil unrest and avoid challenges to state legitimacy. Taken even further are violent actions by the IRA in Northern Ireland, FARC in Colombia and ISIL in the Levant, all establishing that violent revolutionary groups as non-state actors can weaken state sovereignty. These actors directly challenge the legitimacy of a state and thus its sovereignty.

In conclusion, it appears that if non-state actors are included as 'insider' groups (such as trade unions in Scandinavia) and involved in participatory processes, then they can have a positive effect on state sovereignty. However, if they are treated as 'outsider' groups (such with the limited IGO agreement over Syria), or large demographics are ostracized (such as the IRA and FARC), then non-state actors may in fact greatly challenge state sovereignty.

This is the most important question as it is worth approximately 40% of the marks for Paper 1.

ANSWER ANALYSIS

Links are established between the sources, the student's own knowledge and case studies.

ANSWER ANALYSIS

Recent and relevant case studies are used as evidence throughout the response.

AO3: Synthesis and evaluation.

AO4: Use and application of appropriate skills.

ANSWER ANALYSIS

This answer would be worth the full 10 marks.

Paper 2

For your Paper 2 exam you will be given a choice of eight essay questions, two for each unit of study. You can only answer one question per unit of study. If you are studying SL you must answer **two** questions (so two units of study), if you are studying HL you must choose **three** questions (three units of study).

1. To what extent has the concept of state sovereignty evolved in the 21st century?
    [25]

> Sovereignty can be viewed to have evolved in the 21st century due to the increasing limitations placed upon states by IGOs and other non-state actors, which has in turn created increasing interdependence, thus weakening states' legitimacy and power.

DISCUSS/ EVALUATE/TO WHAT EXTENT

These terms will normally be used about issues that have two or more major competing perspectives. This means your responses need to be balanced.

ANSWER ANALYSIS

The key 'hinge' word in this question that you should look at is **evolved**. You should address the role that the question of evolution plays in your response. If you do not focus on the evolving nature of the key concept, sovereignty, you will not be successful.

In order to develop your point from an assertion into an argument, you must explain it further using other relevant keywords (power, legitimacy, interdependence), appropriate vocabulary and relevant knowledge.

Use **PEEA** to structure your answer:

P = A **Point** can be produced at the start of a paragraph, providing an argument in relation to the question.

E = **Explain** your point using additional knowledge, information and vocabulary.

E = **Evidence** your explanation, using factual knowledge relevant to the course and case study examples to create an argument related to the question.

A = **Analyse** your evidence by critiquing and engaging with the argument and evidence presented, which can be from a theoretical perspective.

> With the growing influence of groups such as the UN, IMF, African Union, EU and others displaying greater global interdependence, we can clearly see that these IGO actors in particular are challenging traditional assumptions surrounding state sovereignty in political, economic, military and socio-cultural terms, as well as traditional models of the manifestation of power. In order to become full members of an IGO, often certain levels of state sovereignty must be ceded to the IGO, as they are 'supranational' bodies. Therefore, this challenges a number of the traditional Westphalian concepts related to internal and external sovereignty established by the Treaty of Westphalia in 1648.

ANSWER ANALYSIS

The focus of the question is upon the key term **sovereignty** (one of your sixteen key concepts) and the argument that it has evolved as a concept. Therefore, your introductory point to each paragraph must focus upon this. The other related concepts that could be referred to in the answer are **power, legitimacy** and **interdependence**.

ANSWER ANALYSIS

Here the specificity of knowledge is developed by usage of appropriate dates, groups and terminology.

ANSWER ANALYSIS

In order to verify the argument, it is necessary to provide case study evidence and examples that corroborate the argument being made. In this example, the case studies used are Brexit and the actions of the International Red Cross and Oxfam.

For example, when we explore an IGO, such as the EU from its outset in the early 1950s as an economic trading block, it is evident that large levels of internal economic and internal legal sovereignty have been eroded from member states. Consistent treaty ratifications have led to further political and economic integration of the member states. Recently this challenge to traditional state sovereignty has become an increasing public debate, bringing wider issues regarding overall democratic legitimacy into question, with some public resistance evidenced by the Brexit referendum outcome in 2016 and the rise of populist nationalism across Europe. Indeed, votes across Europe were being attributed to anti-EU 'Populist' parties and the 2019 European Elections saw substantial gains for anti-EU blocks in Hungary, Italy and the UK. NGOs actions can also weaken state sovereignty. NGOs such as the International Red Cross in Syria and Iraq from 2012 to date, or Oxfam in Somalia and Ethiopia in the early to mid-2000s, cut across state boundaries, weakening their external borders and, by extension, their external sovereignty.

Thus contemporary global events point to support for the neo-liberal school of thought, which places primacy upon the increasing influence of interdependence at the expense of autonomous state sovereignty. This establishes that state sovereignty has evolved in the 21st century. Indeed, theorists such as Nye, via his focus upon different forms of power, could argue that not only is sovereignty as a concept evolving in the 21st century, so too is the state's ability to utilize 'hard power', because actors, state and non, are now interdependent. This is most clearly evidenced in the growing usage of 'soft power' or the hybrid 'smart power' in the 21st century, such as China's Belt and Road program across Africa or China's acquisition of ports in Sri Lanka in 2019.

Therefore, there is a clear argument that the concept of sovereignty has evolved in the 21st century to contend with the enhanced role played by IGOs and NGOs.

Remember that Paper 2 requires you to focus upon Assessment Objectives 1–3. Following a PEEA essay structure should help you to focus on these AOs.

There is more than one way to answer an essay question. Below are some examples of other ways you could have approached the question.

ANSWER ANALYSIS

The student rearticulates the argument using the wording of the question at the end of the paragraph. This displays to the examiner the student's focus on the question.

ANSWER ANALYSIS

This paragraph clearly displays evidence of meeting AO1–AO3 skills.

Other ways you could have answered this question

- States are still the dominant actor in the international arena due to the anarchic nature of the international system. The South China Sea territorial conflict and USA vs. Iran rhetoric in 2019 display this. IGOs are comprised of states, therefore their primacy within the international arena is maintained.

- States still manifest both internal and external sovereignty, even when joining and leaving IGOs (for example, Brexit).

- States' inability to execute internal or external sovereignty will often lead to the state become a failing or failed state (Sudan/Somalia). The inability to fully control either internal or external sovereignty will often destabilize to such an extent civil war may happen (Syria/Libya).

- This would correlate with Realist interpretations of international relations including that of Hedley Bull, Kenneth Waltz and John Mearshimer.

- Therefore, states maintain their dominant position within the international system.

- Due to continued globalization and the growth in power of Multinational corporations, state sovereignty has been weakened to the point of being eroded.

- Examples of MNCs using their economic might to bring favourable policies include Nike's actions in Vietnam and Apple's in China. These actions display a weakening of internal economic sovereignty as the state meets the needs of the non-state actors, often creating negative working conditions for labour.

- Developing nations in particular are often very amenable to economic pressures from non-state actors in order to guarantee foreign direct investment from the MNC to allow their economies to grow.

- However, there is a state-centric converse argument, focused upon the role of state-led FDI investments, which displays states as the most important actors, particularly the USA and China.

- Further opportunities for discussion of liberalism and neo-liberalism.

- There is some movement towards non-state nations potentially being legitimized, such as the Kurds across Turkey, Syria and Iraq. International recognition is being given to these groups and there is a growing movement towards their legitimate recognition as their own nation, therefore, weakening traditional models of Westphalian sovereignty already in place.

- Some nations can exist as states, without full internal and external sovereignty, such as Palestine. Palestine does hold UN recognition as an observer state, meaning they do have legitimacy, but they cannot exert external sovereignty, therefore displaying the inappropriate nature of traditional models of statehood.

- However, critically these 'nations' all aspire to statehood and creation thereof, clearly evidencing the state as the primary actor.

TESTING WHAT YOU KNOW

In this section, you will be able to test yourself with different sets of practice papers under exam conditions. By taking these mock papers, you will build your confidence and be able to identify any areas you need a bit more practice on. Set A Paper 1 and Paper 2 have a lot of additional guidance in the margin to help you get to the right answer, so attempt Set A first.

All you need is this book, a timer, a pen and some extra paper to use if you run out of answer lines. Then you can check your answers at the back of the book when you're done.

Take a deep breath, set your timer, and good luck!

Set A

Paper 1: Standard and Higher Level

- Set your timer for **1 hour and 15 minutes**
- The maximum mark for this examination paper is 25 marks
- Answer ALL the questions

Unit 1: Power, sovereignty and international relations

Read all the sources carefully and answer all the questions that follow.

Source A

Graph showing GDP per capita. Adjusted for price changes over time (inflation) and for price difference between countries to allow comparisons – it is measured in international $ in 2011 prices.

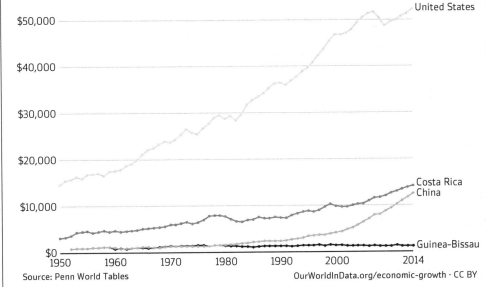

Source: Penn World Tables   OurWorldInData.org/economic-growth · CC BY

> Remember, you will be allowed five minutes of reading time at the start of this exam where you are not allowed to write or highlight!

> The source has already been adjusted for inflation so you can compare the figures.

GDP PER CAPITA

This represents how much a countries economy affects the standard of life.

Source B

Adapted from 'How can you measure what makes a country great', an article by Amanda Ruggeri, www.bbc.co.uk. (2018).

There are typically two measurements used to judge how well a country is doing. One is examining the percentage of how many people are unemployed. The other is looking at how much the country earns (otherwise known as gross domestic product (GDP)). However, despite being the standard method for nearly two hundred years, these measurements may not be helpful when determining how well a country is serving its citizens.

The Social Progress Index can instead be used to see how well a country is serving its population by aggregating data about countries worldwide. This type of index is less well known and is more typically known for lists ranking which countries you might want to move to (with Denmark or New Zealand coming out on top).

Interestingly, when measuring social progress, it can be poorer countries that come out on top. For example, they often have more accessible and affordable education, food and housing compared to their wealthier counterparts. "Broadly, richer countries have higher social progress, so getting more economic growth is not a bad idea," says Michael Green, CEO of the Social Progress Index. "But what we also find, very clearly, is that social progress is not completely explained by economic variables. GDP is not destiny."

AGGREGATING

Collecting a range of information.

ECONOMIC VARIABLES

Measurements that help realize the function of an economy.

DESTINY

Fate, what is meant to be.

[Source: Adapted from an article published on the BBC Ruggeri, A (2018), How can you measure what makes a country great [online]. Retrieved from: www.bbc.com/future/story/20180111-how-can-you-measure-what-makes-a-country-great [Accessed on: 06 November 2019]]

Source C

'Practitioners of Development', a lecture by Professor John Williamson (2004)

Professor John Williamson coined the phrase 'Washington Consensus'.

The ten reforms that constituted his list were as follows.

1. Fiscal discipline
2. Reordering public expenditure priorities
3. Tax reform
4. Liberalizing interest rates
5. A competitive exchange rate
6. Trade liberalization
7. Liberalization of inward foreign direct investment
8. Privatization
9. Deregulation
10. Property rights

[Source: Adapted from a lecture by Professor Williamson in the series 'Practitioners of Development', delivered at the World Bank on January 13, 2004. (Full speech is available at: https://www.piie.com/publications/papers/williamson0204.pdf)]

Source D

An extract from 'Special Report: State Capitalism' by Adrian Wooldridge, published by *The Economist (2012)*

Over the past 15 years striking corporate headquarters have transformed the great cities of the emerging world. China Central Television's building resembles a giant alien marching across Beijing's skyline; the 88-storey Petronas Towers, home to Malaysia's oil company, soar above Kuala Lumpur; the gleaming office of VTB, a banking powerhouse, sits at the heart of Moscow's new financial district. These are all monuments to the rise of a new kind of hybrid corporation, backed by the state but behaving like a private-sector multinational.

State-directed capitalism is not a new idea: witness the East India Company. But as our special report this week points out, it has undergone a dramatic revival. In the 1990s most state-owned companies were little more than government departments in emerging markets; the assumption was that, as the economy matured, the government would close or privatise them. Yet they show no signs of relinquishing the commanding heights, whether in major industries (the world's ten biggest oil-and-gas firms, measured by reserves, are all state-owned) or major markets (state-backed companies account for 80% of the value of China's stock market and 62% of Russia's). And they are on the offensive. Look at almost any new industry and a giant is emerging: China Mobile, for example, has 600m customers. State-backed firms accounted for a third of the emerging world's foreign direct investment in 2003–10.

[Source: Wooldridge, A (2012), "Special Report: State Capitalism", *The Economist*]

1. Outline what Source A tells us about trends in development. **[3]**

If there is a long source, in the margin you could summarize the content to help you with planning for the questions.

HYBRID CORPORATION
Bringing together the best parts of non-profit and for-profit corporations.

RELINQUISHING
To give something up voluntarily.

When looking at trends in development, it is important to examine changes in GDP.

OUTLINE
Outline means to clearly state what is visible in the source. This means you shouldn't waste time evaluating why this is or what it could mean, simply say what is visible.

The first question should be answered in bullet points.

You should quote or refer directly to the source in question.

Only use Source A for this question. You will not get marks for using the other sources too.

2. With explicit reference to Source B and to **one** example you have studied, explain why development is a difficult concept to measure. **[4]**

Source B outlines both economic and human development indicators, establishing the problems with traditional economic focus over human factors.

ANSWER ANALYSIS

In source questions, double check you are looking at the right one. This question is asking about Source B.

A disadvantage of measuring development economically via GDP/GDP per capita/GNP is that they do not account for wealth distribution and do not account for human development factors, making their modern usage somewhat limited.

You could talk about ways of measuring development. These are easiest classified as measurement of economic factors, human factors or hybrid systems.

Question 2 asks you to also discuss another example you have studied. It is not enough to only talk about Source B.

3. Contrast what Source C **and** Source D reveal about pathways to development. **[8]**

The 'Washington Consensus' is a term coined to represent ten actions a state should take towards liberalization, including economic and other policies, in order to enhance its development potential.

State capitalism is when state-owned corporations play major roles in a state's economic development.

Contrast means you need to establish the differences between the two different policies/theories.

Structural Adjustment Policies are required by the World Bank and IMF as a condition of qualifying for loans. They can also be related to policies implemented in the 1980s associated with neo-liberalism.

4. 'Increasing trade liberalization is the only requirement for a state to develop.' Using all the sources **and** your own knowledge, to what extent do you agree with this claim? **[10]**

Trade liberalization is the removal of tariffs and protectionist barriers on capital and goods.

Export orientation is focused upon competitive domestic markets and development and exploitation of these niche areas.

This question has instructed you to refer to all the sources (A–D), so make sure you do so.

If possible, try to apply a case study to each of the individual sources.

You are being asked if you agree with the statement. Whether you agree or disagree, you must include it in your response.

Read the question carefully. It is important you do not miss the word 'only' in the quote.

That's it – your first Paper 1 practice is complete! Don't worry if you went over your timer. Reading the additional tips takes extra time. Make a note of any areas you found difficult and focus on those for your revision in the next few days. Make sure you take a bit of a break – don't go straight into Paper 2. It's important to recharge!

Set A

Paper 2: Standard and Higher Level

SL candidates
- Set your timer for **1 hour and 45 mins**
- There are 50 marks available
- Answer TWO questions from different units of study

HL candidates
- Set your timer for **2 hours and 45 mins**
- There are 75 marks available
- Answer THREE questions from different units of study

Each question is worth 25 marks.

Power, sovereignty and international relations

1. Examine the claim that power in global politics can only be measured in terms of military power. **[25]**

Take the time to plan your answer before starting to write.

In your answer introduction show your knowledge of the concept to illustrate you understand the question.

You could consider the reasons some people think they know what is best for others.

Don't forget to include case studies. Recent military conflicts might be good examples.

Have you thought about how military power could be measured?

You could consider Joseph Nye's theory on power.

Focus on the key hinge word in the question, 'measured' in significant detail. You could underline it to keep you focused while you answer. Think about whether or not power in global politics can only be measured in terms of military power.

Use case studies which can be applied on different levels of analysis.

Don't forget about PEEA:
- P = Point
- E = Explain
- E = Evidence
- A = Analyse

All paper 2 questions test AO1, AO2, AO3 and AO4.

Be careful to avoid the common errors students make confusing sovereignty and legitimacy. To help you remember you could consider legitimacy as consent to act and sovereignty as legal jurisdiction over territory.

2. To what extent do you agree that unilateral state actions limit global governance? **[25]**

Don't forget that this unit focuses on power, sovereignty, legitimacy and interdependence. However, you are not restricted to only using information from the first unit.

You could consider the view of neo-liberals towards states taking unilateral actions.

Don't forget to include case studies. For example, you could talk about the Paris Climate Accords.

 TO WHAT EXTENT

This means you need to use your evidence and discussion to decide how much you agree.

You can use examples of intergovernmental organizations (such as the World Bank) to explore the question.

You might want to consider the advantages/disadvantages of multi-lateral actions in your answer.

The key hinge word in this question is 'limit'. Your answer must focus on this in order to access the highest markband.

Do not spend too long describing multi-lateral actions. It can be a useful comparison but the question has asked about your opinion of unilateral actions.

ANSWER ANALYSIS

You are also being tested on your ability to write an argument that is easy to follow: use paragraphs and link your points in a logical way.

Always have an evaluative conclusion that clearly answers the question.

Remember to refer to the key theories and the viewpoints they offer to show different perspectives and counter claims.

Human rights

3. 'The Universal Declaration of Human Rights (1948) displays a Western attitude towards Human Rights, at the expense of other non-Western perspectives.' Discuss this statement.   [25]

How do we decide which experts to follow when they make different claims?

Human rights are based on values such as dignity, equality and independence. They belong to every person regardless of factors such as location, age or position in society.

Three important perspectives are gender, ethnicity and religion. Remember to link back to the question at the beginning of your answer. Talk about why the UDHR might be considered to reflect a Western perspective.

DISCUSS

Outline the similarities and differences between viewpoints.

You could explore China's focus on collective or group rights as your contemporary example. Or what about Female Genital Mutilation in Uganda?

Make a note or highlight this unit in the EXPLAIN section if you are struggling to recall relevant terminology or case studies. This will help you to decide what to focus on when you revise.

If you are struggling to think of appropriate case studies, write about what you know from your own context; what might be a well-known case study for a student in the Philippines might be totally different from a student in Hong Kong. Examiners will appreciate a variety and difference in the case studies they see.

Remember you can apply some case studies across multiple topics (for example, Yemen could be in Peace and Conflict, Development and Human Rights).

4. Discuss how cultural relativism impacts upon the notion of human rights. **[25]**

Cultural relativism means cultural differences should be considered in human rights. Non-Western societies have different levels of development and histories, for example.

If you are using a gender perspective, remember that this form of identity can be biologically determined or socially constructed. Many issues in human rights are highly gendered.

Remember that human rights are, by definition, universal. Universalists argue that these rights belong to everyone and should not be affected by culture.

Keep an eye on the clock. Don't use all your time on this one question.

Your answer must demonstrate in-depth understanding of your case studies.

It might be argued that it is a child's right to go to school. However, this can conflict with the community's opinion if the children are needed to help at home or will likely grow up to do manual work.

You might consider how religious beliefs conflict with human rights. Female genital mutilation is an example of this.

ANSWER ANALYSIS

When you make a point, you must relate it back to the question being asked. And, for each point, you need to back it up with appropriate evidence.

The difference between detailed case studies and general examples is in the fine points such as names, places and statistics. Revise these carefully.

Development

5. Evaluate the claim that development goals, such as the Millennium and Sustainable Development Goals, will never be achieved, unless coherency in both measurement and action is achieved. **[25]**

....

....

....

....

....

....

....

....

....

....

....

....

....

....

....

....

....

....

....

....

....

....

....

....

....

....

....

This unit includes different perspectives upon development, globalization, inequality and sustainability.

The Millennium Development Goals established a global set of important social priorities worldwide.

The Sustainable Development Goals were adopted by the United Nation Members States in 2015 as steps towards a more sustainable future by 2030.

Make sure you are answering the question. Don't go off on a tangent describing every single thing you know about the unit.

Global goals involve different states, which have different attitudes and priorities.

Reread the question and make sure you understand what it is asking before you attempt to answer it.

ANSWER ANALYSIS

To get the highest marks for this question, you will need to consider both how you agree and disagree with the claim.

Consider the competing perspectives around development measures (for example, modernization and dependency theory).

ANSWER ANALYSIS

To get the highest marks you need to demonstrate a good grasp of the key concepts of the course. For this question this relates to globalization, poverty and inequality.

When you are revising for Paper 2 make sure you look at the prescribed content from the subject guide as this is where the questions will come from.

6. Discuss the view that without political stability sustained development cannot be achieved. **[25]**

ANSWER ANALYSIS

Make sure to maintain your focus on the question throughout your response. Examiners expect to see a clear 'thread' – a logical movement from point to point throughout the essay, which is academically structured, with an appropriate introduction, main body and conclusion.

Plan your essay paragraphs using PEEA to access all four of the assessment objectives.

Political factors can play a substantial role in a state's economic and human development. Think about which sub issues these political factors can often be broken down into.

Global politics case studies must be from within your lifetime. For example, you could talk about the civil war in Yemen.

Global politics is ever evolving; check the news headlines every day for case studies and events you can include.

Include competing theories and perspectives.

Conclusions should directly answer the question.

Paper 2 questions 1–8 tests all four assessment objectives.

EVALUATE

'Evaluate' requires you to critique the claim given.

Make clear references to the keywords in the question in each essay. You should try to refer to these at the end of each paragraph to build up an argument.

A conclusion is not a simple summary of the arguments you have presented. It is a clear judgment given by you on the question set, considering all of the knowledge, evidence and theories articulated in your response.

Peace and conflict

7. 'Identity is now more important than resources in causing violent conflict.'
Discuss this claim with reference to either an interstate or intrastate conflict
you have studied. **[25]**

If using a religious perspective, remember that religious identity can have both a personal and social aspect. It can explain life and meaning to an individual, but that individual is often part of a religious community and follows their rules and customs too.

Don't forget to include an interstate or intrastate conflict in your response. You should integrate it into your answer.

To demonstrate your understanding of violent conflict you could discuss how it has changed from in the past to today.

You could also discuss how the changing face of violent conflict has also changed which actors are involved and why.

You could use the Kurdish conflict as an example.

ANSWER ANALYSIS

You should examine how you agree and how you disagree with the statement in order to present a balanced argument. Remember, there are two sides to every argument.

8. Examine the claim that positive peace is unobtainable. [25]

ANSWER ANALYSIS

Detailed case study examples must be used to drive forward the essay. This displays key knowledge of the course content, theoretical foundations and their application to a real-world context. On this occasion Chad, Colombia and Northern Ireland are all good case studies.

Use different levels of analysis to provide sustained evaluation.

Discuss the key concepts associated with this unit; peace, conflict, violence and non-violence.

Integration of theories can provide a theoretical context.

You can use a case study more than once, but make sure that you are applying it in a different context of discussion.

The essay should take you 52–55 minutes to plan and write.

Briefly using knowledge across units is a good skill. However, some candidates become distracted and focus too much upon different units rather than the one in question. Avoid this! Stay focused on the question in particular.

EXAMINE

'Examine' is the command term used; this requires you to critique the claim given.

ANSWER ANALYSIS

It is not enough to just list counterclaims. You must be able to explore them.

Set B

Are you ready to tackle Set B? There are fewer helpful tips and suggestions for this set so make sure you have done some revision before you try out these two papers.

Take at least a day's break between Paper 1 and Paper 2. Don't burn yourself out.

Have you remembered extra paper in case you run out of space?

Paper 1: Standard and Higher Level

- Set your timer for **1 hour and 15 minutes**
- The maximum mark for this examination paper is 25 marks
- Answer ALL the questions

Unit 3: Development

Read all the sources carefully and answer all the questions that follow.

Source A

Literacy rate by country for the entire global population, 2011

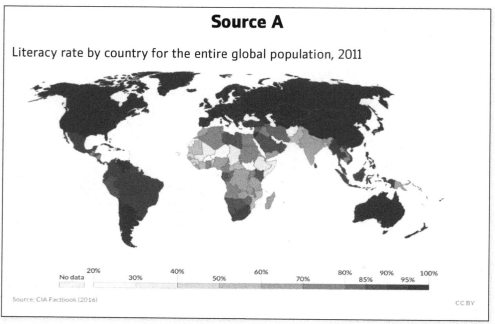

Source: CIA Factbook (2016)   CC BY

[Source: CIA Factbook, 2016]

Source B

Adapted from 'Can political stability hurt economic growth?', a blog article written by Zahad Hussain (2014)

Conflict and rife competition between political parties – the very definition of political instability – can lead to state collapse. Changes to states can not only be disruptive but also often lead to more change. Political instability breeds more political instability in a relentless cycle.

The connection between political instability and poor economic growth is deep-rooted. Political instability causes a lack of certainty which, in turn, can cause a shrinking of investment and can slow economic growth. The reverse can also happen. A slow-down in economic growth could lead to political instability and the collapse of states.

Political stability isn't only achieved through positive means, however. A state with an oppressed population might still be stable. So might a state with a political party in power that had no rival.

Therefore, political stability can come at a price. States that have unchecked and unrestricted power to give friends and trusted associates positions of power can exist without consequences. What a problem to be faced by countries in precarious political situations.

[Source: Adapted from a blog article: Hussain, Z. (2014), "Can political stability hurt economic growth?", World Bank Blogs. [online]. Retrieved from: blogs.worldbank.org/endpovertyinsouthasia/can-political-stability-hurt-economic-growth [Accessed on: 05 December 2019]]

Source C

Report of the UN Committee for Development Policy (2019)

On the Economic and Social Council theme, the Committee emphasized that current levels of inequality were unacceptable and unsustainable. Moving towards inclusiveness and equality requires overturning processes that disempower people and communities. Development under unfettered market conditions and poor institutional frameworks can be disempowering when people are excluded or when participation in productive systems is under conditions that would leave people vulnerable, such as unpaid work. Climate change risks are a major factor in the disempowerment of communities, directly and through the additional burden they place on the resources of the poorest Governments. This combination of factors not only clashes with the ideals of social justice, equity and sustainability, but also fuels conflict and insecurity. With little more than a decade left for the implementation of the 2030 Agenda, and with the pressing challenges and risks posed by climate change, there is an urgent need to rethink the factors that determine the direction of investment and innovation; the terms under which people are included in production, consumption and financial systems; and the distribution of the benefits, costs and risks of economic activity. There is a window of opportunity for a transformation grounded in equality, inclusion and human rights, where both the empowerment of those at risk of being left or pushed behind and the mechanisms that enable the concentration of wealth and power at the top are addressed.

Economic and Social Council (2019), Report of the UN Committee for Development Policy [online]. Supplement: 13. Retrieved from: undocs.org/en/E/2019/33 [Accessed on: 05 December 2019]]

Source D

Adapted from the OECD article 'Why Open Markets Matter' (2019)

Trade has contributed to lifting hundreds of millions of people out of poverty: the share of the world's population living on less than PPP USD 1.90 per day fell from around 35% in 1990 to less than 10% in 2015. Evidence on the impact of trade on poverty in developing countries from 1993 to 2008 shows that the change in the real income of the bottom 20% of the population is strongly correlated with the change in trade openness over the same period. Developing and emerging economies are playing a more important role today in trade than ever before, contributing to declining inequality among countries (though not always within countries).

Trade has delivered unprecedented access to goods and services, with a revolution in the availability of goods for low income households.

UNSUSTAINABLE
Cannot be maintained at the the current level.

DISEMPOWER
Take away someone's control and power.

UNFETTERED
Unrestricted

INNOVATION
To think creatively, a new idea, or method.

CORRELATED
Links and connects to something.

UNPRECEDENTED
Never done before

REVOLUTION
Going against a government in order to gain a new system.

Take the cost of purchasing a television set, for example: between 1980 and 2014, the price of a roughly comparable TV set fell by 73%, in part as the result of ambitious trade liberalisation efforts – and the smart television sets we buy today are vastly better than those available in the 1980s. Lower prices are particularly beneficial for poor households, which spend relatively more on heavily-traded products (for example, staples such as food and garments).

[Source: OECD (2019), Why Open Markets Matter [online]. Retrieved from: www.oecd.org/trade/understanding-the-global-trading-system/why-open-markets-matter/]

1. Outline what Source A identifies about how literacy rates can influence development. [3]

The first question should be answered in bullet points.

When looking at development, it is important to consider human development factors such as education.

A link needs to be drawn between literacy and development. Often states with higher standards of educational provision will develop further economically.

The source has already been adjusted for inflation so you can compare the figures.

2. With explicit reference to Source B and to **one** example you have studied, explain why political factors may promote development. [4]

Political factors and their promotion of development is stated in the question. Focus on this.

Political factors affecting development are often sub-categorized into conflict, ideology and governance.

Case studies to develop here could include conflict in Yemen, ideology in Nigeria and corruption in Venezuela.

Make it clear to the examiner when you are using your own example. You could use language like "an example of this is…"

3. Contrast what Source C **and** Source D reveal about the impact social issues can have on development. **[8]**

....

....

....

....

....

....

....

....

....

....

....

....

....

....

....

....

....

....

....

The origin of the sources must always be considered. Source C is from the UN and Source D the OECD. This in part establishes the difference between the arguments.

Use specific quotations from each source to evidence the statement you make to get the marks.

Corroborate the statement and source work with your own knowledge of case studies and course knowledge.

4. 'Economic factors are the most important criteria when a state is seeking to develop.' With reference to all the sources **and** your own knowledge, to what extent do you agree with this claim? **[10]**

....

....

....

....

....

....

....

....

....

....

....

....

....

The argument will have competing perspectives, be sure to include both.

Using the sources in combination is a strong skill to display.

ANSWER ANALYSIS

This question requires 3–4 paragraphs as a response.

Be sure to make four separate comparisons. When you quote be clear in your answer by stating which source you are using.

Remember that question 4 is a mini paper 2 essay so include key global politics theories, levels of analysis and perspectives.

Set B

Paper 2: Standard and Higher Level

SL candidate
- Set your timer for **1 hour and 45 mins**
- There are 50 marks available
- Answer TWO questions from different units of study

HL candidate
- Set your timer for **2 hours and 45 mins**
- There are 75 marks available
- Answer THREE questions from different units of study

Each question is worth 25 marks.

Power, sovereignty and international relations

1. Evaluate the claim that the link between control of resources and power is diminishing. **[25]**

ANSWER ANALYSIS

Make a plan and refer back to it regularly when writing your answer.

Remember that resources can be raw materials or digital.

Consider how you would define power: there are different types.

An example of a case study could be the conflict in the South China Sea (2019).

In your answer introduction show your knowledge of the concept to illustrate you understand the question.

Be careful to avoid the common errors students make confusing sovereignty and legitimacy. To help you remember you could consider legitimacy as consent to act and sovereignty as legal jurisdiction over territory.

2. To what extent do you agree that intrastate conflict is more damaging to a regime than interstate conflict? [25]

Human rights

3. Evaluate the key challenges in upholding human rights. [25]

Before you can look at the challenges in upholding human rights, you must demonstrate your understanding of them.

Consider the United Nationals Human Rights Council.

ANSWER ANALYSIS

Check you have included case studies that are relevant and from within your lifetime. Ensure you have integrated them into your answer.

4. 'Universal human rights will never be practically achieved, due to individual states's pursuit of power.' Discuss the validity of this statement. **[25]**

Consider Universalism when attempting this question. Define the term as part of your answer.

Consider how a state's attitude towards human rights will affect their image, both to outsiders and locally.

You could use examples of past applications of human rights, and where they have succeeded and failed.

Avoid phrases like 'I believe' and write in third person. This means using phrases such as 'Another viewpoint argues...'.

Development

5. Evaluate the claim that poverty is primarily caused by improper governance.

[25]

Plan your answer before starting to write it, and then refer back to it regularly.

ANSWER ANALYSIS

You will only get the highest marks if you consider both sides of the argument.

ANSWER ANALYSIS

After discussing both viewpoints, you must evaluate which presents the most compelling evidence.

Check you are answering the question throughout and not adding irrelevant information.

6. To what extent have the negative outcomes of globalization outweighed
    the positive?   [25]

....

....

....

....

....

....

....

....

....

....

....

....

....

....

....

....

....

....

....

....

....

....

....

....

....

....

....

....

....

....

....

....

You must use relevant and contemporary examples from the real world in your answer.

ANSWER ANALYSIS

Ensure you make it clear how any examples you include are relevant to your argument.

ANSWER ANALYSIS

End your answer with a conclusion of your most important points and an answer to the question.

In order to answer the question properly you will need to discuss what the negative and positive outcomes are, and then decide which is more valuable.

Don't just list opposing viewpoints. You must go into some depth to get marks for including them.

Peace and conflict

7. 'The legitimate usage of violence can only ever be claimed by the state.'
   Discuss the validity of this claim. **[25]**

You must analyse the political issues in case studies.

If you are struggling with a topic then make a note to revise it further.

Decide what your line of argument is going to be so you can remain consistent throughout the essay.

ANSWER ANALYSIS

Ensure your argument is balanced. Even if you do not agree, you should show that you have considered opposing viewpoints.

Case studies are important but they should not overpower your main point.

8. Discuss to what extent peacemaking, peacekeeping and peace building are interrelated concepts. **[25]**

ANSWER ANALYSIS

You could start the essay by defining the key concept. This shows that you understand it and it will help you to start writing.

Keep on topic. Only include something if it is relevant to your argument.

When planning your essay, decide which theories you will use and how they will help you to make your point.

It is **global** politics, so your case studies should come from more than one country.

Set C

This set of papers has no additional help in the margins. There is a space to write notes so you can plan what you are going to write if needed.

Paper 1: Standard and Higher Level

- Set your timer for **1 hour and 15 minutes**
- The maximum mark for this examination paper is 25 marks
- Answer ALL the questions

Unit 2: Human rights

Read all the sources carefully and answer all the questions that follow.

Source A

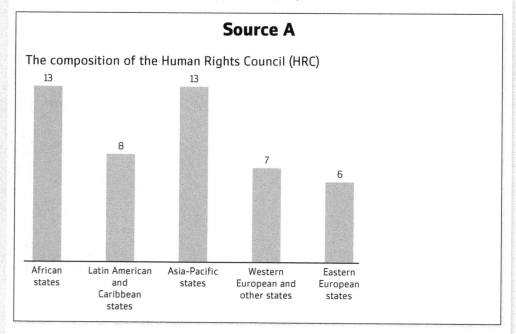

The composition of the Human Rights Council (HRC)

Category	Value
African states	13
Latin American and Caribbean states	8
Asia-Pacific states	13
Western European and other states	7
Eastern European states	6

Source B

Extract from 'Human Rights' in The *Globalization of World Politics* by Jack Donnelly (2017)

The Human Rights Council has established a system of universal periodic review. Because the reviewers are states rather than independent experts, however, the typical review is often somewhat less penetrating. Furthermore, the universal scope of the procedure results in reports of widely varying depth and breadth. Nonetheless, in some instances significant monitoring does occur...

[Source: Donnelly, J (2017), Human Rights, in: Bayliss, J, et al., The Globalization of World Politics, 7th Ed. Oxford: Oxford University Press, p. 500]

PERIODIC REVIEW

Evaluation on a regular basis.

PENETRATING

Invasive, thorough

Source C

Extract from a journal article called 'The Global Politics of Human Rights: From Human Rights to Human Dignity?' by Salvador Santino F Regilme (2019)

[...] the deep ideological divisions during the Cold War era facilitated human rights activism within and beyond the American policy establishment, yet other American stakeholders also permitted the

IDEALOGICAL DIVISIONS

Differences in ideas or beliefs.

pervasive abuses of US allies for the sake of US interests. Second, the complexity of US foreign policy construction was aggravated by a 'high degree of politicization, and even opportunism' (Renouard, 2015: 15). That may be the case when American politicians and policymakers strategically deployed 'human rights' discourses to score winning political advantages – particularly in debates in the US Congress, on foreign aid, democracy promotion initiatives and other policy spheres in US external relations. Third, US foreign policy and its human rights outcomes cannot be accurately interpreted by any single theoretical framework, because 'there were simply too many unique cases worldwide and too many interests driving American involvement' [...]

[Source: Regilme, S. S. F. (2019), "The Global Politics of Human Rights: From Human Rights to Human Dignity?", International Political Science Review, Volume 40, Issue 2, pp. 279 -290]

PERVASIVE

Widespread and invasive.

AGGRAVATED

To make worse.

Source D

Extract from a Journal article called 'Documentation: International Legal Human Rights Framework: Human Rights and the Institutionalisation of ASEAN: An Ambiguous Relationship' by Theodor Rathgeber (2014)

[...] it may be said that the development of the human rights situation in the ten member states reveals an institutional process that aims to reform structural elements of governance irrespective of the diversity of implementation processes. The process related to human rights standards leaves governance open to challenge by internationally agreed-upon (human rights) law standards and language [...] With regard to the core human rights treaties, there is much room for ASEAN countries to accede to the full range of these treaties – beyond the CEDAW and CRC, to which all are party. All ASEAN countries have participated in the Universal Periodic Review and principally accepted the rules. ASEAN states were less open-minded with regard to being monitored by the Special Procedures, though the Special Rapporteurs are a key component in ensuring human rights. An effective and comprehensive human rights protection system is absent in every country of the region and in ASEAN itself.

[Source: Rathgeber, T (2014), "Documentation: International Legal Human Rights Framework: Human Rights and the Institutionalisation of ASEAN: An Ambiguous Relationship", Journal of Current Southeast Asian Affairs, Volume 33, Issue 3, pp. 131–165]

IRRESPECTIVE

Not taking into consideration.

IMPLEMENTATION

Putting a plan into action.

ASEAN

Association of South East Asian Nations

CEDAW

Convention on the Elimination of All Forms of Discrimination Against Women

CRC

Cyclic redundancy check

ACCEDE

To agree to demands.

1. Using Source A, identify **three** features of the Human Rights Council. **[3]**

....
....
....
....
....
....
....
....
....
....
....

SPECIAL RAPPORTEURS

Someone working to rectify specific human rights issues.

2. With explicit reference to Source B and to **one** example you have studied, explain how human rights can be protected. [4]

3. Using Sources C **and** D, contrast the factors that challenge the protection of human rights. [8]

4. Using all of the sources **and** your own knowledge, discuss the impact of politicization of human rights. **[10]**

NOTES

Set C

Paper 2: Standard and Higher Level

SL candidates
- Set your timer for **1 hour and 45 mins**
- There are 50 marks available
- Answer TWO questions from different units of study

HL candidates
- Set your timer for **2 hours and 45 mins**
- There are 75 marks available
- Answer THREE questions from different units of study

Each question is worth 25 marks.

Power, sovereignty and international relations

1. Discuss the impact of non-governmental organizations (NGOs), multinational corporations (MNCs) and trade unions on global politics. **[25]**

NOTES

NOTES

2. 'Soft power is only effective if it is married with hard power.' How far do you agree with this statement? [25]

NOTES

Human rights

3. Discuss whether human rights laws and treaties have enhanced the ability of states to protect human rights. [25]

NOTES

Human rights

3. Discuss whether human rights laws and treaties have enhanced the ability of states to protect human rights.

4. 'Interdependence between states and non-state actors is essential in maintaining the effectiveness of human rights laws.' Evaluate this statement. [25]

NOTES

Development

5. 'Environment and sustainability are now more critical considerations for development than economic and political factors.' Evaluate this view. **[25]**

NOTES

NOTES

6. Evaluate the claim that intergovernmental organizations (IGOs) have a limited effect on development. [25]

NOTES

Peace and conflict

7. Evaluate the claim that 'states are largely responsible for conflict'. [25]

NOTES

NOTES

8. To what extent do you agree with the claim that peace is impossible while there are conditions of structural violence? [25]

NOTES

NOTES

Answers

Set A

Paper 1

1. • Describe the upward trend in GDP per capita figures from 1950–2014, with three of the four states (USA, China and Costa Rica) all evidencing GDP per capita growth. One state displays GDP per capita stagnation across the period (Guinea).
   • The disparity between states as shown in Source A displays sustained GDP growth, but from differing beginnings. Costa Rica's growth is more than two-fold, GDP per capita rising from approximately $5,000 in 1950 to $12,000 in 2014. US GDP per capita rose from approx. $15,000 in 1950 to $50,000 in 2014, more than a three-fold increase. China's growth has been the greatest; from approximately $1,000 in 1950 to approximately $10,000 in 2014, a ten-fold increase.
   • Therefore, the evidence would suggest that over a long time period most states experience economic development. **[3 marks]**

2. • Explain the competing measurements of development outlined in Source B:
     – GDP and unemployment rates are considered purely economic development indicators.
     – The SPI is a human development index and therefore takes account of largely non-economic factors, such as education, housing and healthcare.
   • Therefore, the two forms of development measurement reflect both competing priorities and theoretical bases. The traditional mainstream perspective places priority upon capital preservation and creation (economic development), whilst the other prioritizes human development factors.
   • Examples from studies of China's economic development post 1990 or that of the USA post 1960 are pertinent. However, these can be juxtaposed against both China and the USA's poor performance on the SPI, which would place Sweden, Denmark and Norway significantly above both, despite smaller GDPs. This is because citizens have access to high-quality, state-provided education and healthcare, more progressive workplace policies and greater wealth distribution. **[4 marks]**

3. • Identification of what each source represents:
     – Source C reflects a simplification of the policies commonly known as 'The Washington Consensus'
     – Source D reflects state capitalism.
   • Outlining of the different stances each takes to development. The 'Washington Consensus has been influenced by neo-liberalism's focus upon open competition, free markets, limited state intervention, comparative advantage, individual self-interest, privatization of state enterprises and deregulation.
   • State capitalism on the other hand is a rejection of limited state intervention. Examples of this come from Norway (The Fund) and Sweden's use of sovereign wealth funds, alongside Saudi Arabian (Aramco), Qatari (Qatar Gas) and Malaysian (CNPC) state-owned companies. These actors of state capitalism play major roles in the individual market places.
   • Discussion of the success of Chinese/Russian economic policies is also relevant. Both states have established significant economic growth via aspects of the state capitalism system. **[8 marks]**

4. • Establish understanding of the two key terms:
     – Trade liberalization is the removal of trade barriers, allowing greater competition in the national marketplace from external sources, which will often lead to increased foreign direct investment into a state.
     – Export orientation is the focus upon sectors or industries in which the state has a competitive advantage, with the aim of expanding their exports in this area.
   • Both of these policies are largely tied to the neo-liberal school of thought and so this should be referenced as the theory helped to develop the 'Washington Consensus' and the Structural Adjustment Policies.
   • Source A can be used as evidence for the success of these policies, with GDP per capita growth of the USA, paired with the usage of the ten components of the 'Washington Consensus' in Source C.

   • Evidence drawn from the course may include the role of international organizations such as the International Monetary Fund, World Trade Organization and World Bank.
   • Mainstream definitions of development and the potential linking of raw materials and GDP to a state's potential to execute 'hard power' would also be relevant.
   • However, the claim does not take account of more nuanced perspectives on development. For example, the data in Source A follows a 'one country two systems' approach. Source B represents the increasing importance of social factors in measuring a state's development and Source D establishes the primacy of the role of the state via state capitalism in development.
   • Examples of other mechanisms to develop economies exist, such as capability theory, state capitalism or the creation of a 'knowledge economy'.
   • Environmental factors and building a sustainable economy could also be developed.
   • Strong responses will take account of the mainstream traditional perspective given in the claim. However, they will also critique through a lens of competing theories visible in sources B–D, accompanied with specific knowledge drawn from the course as outlined above. **[10 marks]**

Paper 2

> **Level/marks breakdown for all Paper 2 answers:**
> • Level 2 [6–10 marks] show understanding of the question's key concepts
> • Level 3 [11–15 marks] discuss counter claims
> • Level 4 [16–20 marks] include accurate real-world examples and thoroughly analyse counter claims
> • Level 5 [21–25 marks] include case studies and perspectives and evaluate the concepts in a coherent, structured way

1. Have you remembered and thought about the following in your answer?
   • Power, sovereignty and international relations is a unit of study that includes focus upon power, sovereignty, legitimacy and interdependence.
   • Power as a key concept weaves through all the units of study and fundamentally underpins these units. Joseph Nye and hard/soft/smart are all valid discussions. [Links to question]
   • Power as a key concept is measureable to some theorists, based upon military might, natural resources and manpower, etc. [Defines term and stated perspective]
   • Alternatively, a variety of other conceptions of power exist in modern global politics, which disagree that power is tangible or measurable, especially in a purely military sense. [Correct focus upon 'Examine' question stem]
   • A contemporary example of this would be military spending as a percentage of GDP, which would place the USA significantly ahead of other states in terms of military capacity. [Link to case study]
   • Further exploration of military spending, military conflicts and usage of 'hard power'.

   Discussion points:
   • Full exploration of the concept of power, including the theoretical premises of realism and neo-realism (Mearshimer), neo-liberalism (Nye) and non-mainstream critical theories (Gramsci), etc.
   • Articulation of the competing perspectives around power, including hard vs. soft, economic, military and socio cultural; individual vs. collective; unilateral vs. multilateral. [Considering the 'Examine' stem in the question]
   • It is necessary to consider power on different levels of analysis (global, international, regional, national, local and community).
   • This includes how power can impact upon sovereignty, legitimacy and interdependence. [Key concept focus]
   • Linkage of case study examples. Recent examples could include:
   • the Iranian oil conflict (summer 2019)
     – Syria war (2012–2013)
     – Arab Spring, Iraq and Afghan Wars (2003–2012)
     – Israel–Lebanon War (2006). **[25 marks]**

2. Have you remembered and thought about the following in your answer?

- Power, sovereignty and international relations is a unit of study that includes focus upon power, sovereignty, legitimacy and interdependence.
- International relations and the key concept of interdependence are included within this unit. [Links to question]
- Interdependence can be articulated as when groups and actors within global politics hold shared interests, which creates networks of reliance on a global scale. To some theorists (neo-liberals) this interdependence is often weakened when states take unilateral action, as it upsets the established international community. The usage of evidence relating to the deepening of global governance via IGOs, treaties and conventions or strategic alliances would all establish this. [Defines term and stated perspective]
- Alternatively, other theorists argue that unilateral state action is actually the norm, that state self-interest will always override any form of group concern. Therefore, despite recent moves to deepen global governance via treaties and protocols, states remain the sovereign entities and their engagement with the nuances of global governance varies from issue to issue. Judgments directed towards 'To what extent' required. [Correct focus upon 'To what extent' question stem]
- A contemporary example of this would be the Paris Climate Accords, known officially as the UNFCC, a major diplomatic milestone reached by the global community in 2016. This created international norms related to greenhouse gas emissions and other key environmental standards on a global basis for the first time. This would evidence the strengthening of the global governance regime, with international norms becoming embedded due to multi-lateral actions. [Link to case study]
- However, actions taken unilaterally by certain states in rescinding their agreement to the Accords would display a weakening of the international norms established and thus of global governance itself.

Discussion points:
- Full exploration of the concept of interdependence and global governance via IGOs such as the UN, WTO, IMF, World Bank and others would establish primacy of multi-lateral actions in global governance.
- Discussion of notion of collective security, which can only be achieved by multi-lateral, rather than unilateral, actions. [Considering the 'To what extent' stem in the question]
- Global level of analysis would allow a strong critique of global governance on truly global issues such as nuclear capacity with the lapsing of INF Treaty in February 2019 and Iranian intentions to develop centrifuges from September 2019. [global, international, regional, national and community]
- Interdependence can therefore be both established and rebutted. [Key concept focus]
- Linkage of case study examples. Examples of multi-lateral strengthening of global governance could include treaties creating international Human Rights law, such as the UDHR (1949) and ICCPR (1976) or reactions via the WHO to the Ebola crisis in West Africa starting in 2014. In opposition, the UK/USA military strategic alliance leading to the Iraq and Afghan wars in the 2000s would display an attempt at creating multi-lateralism that failed, the growing public discord for IGOs evident in the UK Brexit crisis in September/October 2019 or China's growing influence in Africa via non IGOs all display unilateral actions hindering global governance. **[25 marks]**

3. Have you remembered and thought about the following in your answer?

- Human rights is a unit of study that includes different perspectives upon human rights, liberty, equality and justice.
- The UDHR (1948) is considered to reflect a Western perspective on human rights, which largely charts the development of European and North American Societies. [Links to question]
- The UDHR (1948) attempted to create universal legal recognition for this perspective on human rights. Western perspective origins are in liberal philosophies and economic progression via industrial revolutions. [Defines term]
- However, there are alternative perspectives that do not agree with the UDHR Western focus. [Correct focus on the 'Discuss' question stem]
- A contemporary example of this is China's focus upon collective and group rights. [Link to case study]
- Further exploration of China and its embodiment of collective rights of the state over individual rights, specifically related to Uighur education camps. [Case study focus]

Discussion points:
- Full exploration of the Western viewpoint associated with UDHR (1948) and other relevant treaties and covenants post 1948 to date. [Answering question]
- Articulation of the non-Western perspectives largely associated with cultural relativism, which challenges the very nature of this perspective and its legal framework. [Considering the second view in the question]
- The politicization of rights nationally, regionally, etc. and problematic situations for states and their functions. [Consideration of different levels of analysis]
- Linkage of case study examples (China, Saudi Arabia, Uganda, Female Genital Mutilation, etc.). **[25 marks]**

4. Have you remembered and thought about the following in your answer?

- Human Rights is a unit of study that includes different perspectives upon human rights, liberty, equality and justice.
- Cultural relativism is often used as a critical position via which to undermine the universalism related to human rights as a concept. [Links to question]
- Cultural relativism articulates that cultures must be understood within their own context, they should not be compared against other cultures; their knowledge and social practices are individualistic cultural practices which must be respected. [Defines term]
- This would directly challenge the universalism assumptions associated with human rights especially within the Western European contextual narrative of the drafting of the UDHR (1948). The ethno centrism implicit in large aspects of the document is at odds with basis of cultural relativism. [Correct focus on the 'Discuss' question stem]
- A contemporary example of this could be polygamy. In 2000, a UN Human Rights Committee found polygamy to be in breach of the International Covenant on Civil and Political Rights. [Link to case study]
- Further exploration of polygamy as an issue. Legal in 58 of 195 states, it is now considered by some to be a breach of certain human rights. This embodies the ethno centrism associated with universal aspects of human rights, as the majority of polygamist states are African or Arab Muslim. [Case study focus]

Discussion points:
- Full exploration of cultural relativism as a concept. [Answering question]
- Cultural relativism tends to equate more clearly with group rights. Perhaps the focus on 3rd generation rights in the latter half of the 20th century reflects this focus.
- Community, local and national levels of analysis can be used to contrast with international and global, bringing strong analysis. [Consideration of different levels of analysis]
- Linkage of case study examples could include female genital mutilation, women's rights or child labour. States in focus could be Indonesia, Algeria, Gabon or Saudi Arabia. **[25 marks]**

5. Have you remembered and thought about the following in your answer?

- Development is a unit of study that includes different perspectives upon development, globalization, inequality and sustainability.
- The Millennium and Sustainable Development Goals are goals against which nations can be judged to have made progress in terms of development, however, conflict can arise when the focus is placed upon different forms of measurement and specific actions taken to achieve this progress. [Links to question]
- The Millennium and Sustainable Development Goals are aims using benchmark indicators (can outline several of these). [Defines term]
- However, there is no agreement upon which of the indictors is the most important, therefore competing perspectives arise as to what actions should be taken by states and how to measure their progress towards development. In addition, there is no agreement as to what actually defines development. [Correct focus upon 'Evaluate' question stem]
- A contemporary example of this is China's focus upon GNP/GDP vs. NGO usage of the Human Development Index, emplifying this basic lack of cohesion. [Link to case study]
- Further exploration of regional or national progression to achieving the Millennium and Sustainable Development Goals. [Case study focus]

Discussion points:
- Full exploration of the Millennium and Sustainable Development Goals, specifically regarding their aims, time frame, etc. [Answering question]

- Articulation of the competing perspectives around development measurement, including modernization theory, dependency theory, neo-liberalism and the Structural Adjustment Policies. [Considering the 'Evaluate' stem in the question]
- The difficulty in achieving consensus of action is largely due to the competing theoretical undercurrent, but also because of the varied geopolitical context. [Consideration of different levels of analysis].
- This includes differences of attitude and action by states related to globalization, poverty and inequality. [Key concept focus]
- Linkage of case study examples (International, regional and national progress towards achievement of the Millennium and Sustainable Development Goals alongside other case studies, which have been studied). **[25 marks]**

6. Have you remembered and thought about the following in your answer?
   - Development is a unit of study that includes different perspectives upon development, globalization, inequality and sustainability.
   - Political factors can play a substantial role in a state's economic and human development. These political factors can often be broken down into sub issues focused upon conflict, ideology and economic system and governance. [Links to question]
   - Development can be measured using economic and human measures, however, conflict, ideological division and the role of state intervention can all affect political stability and thus a state's development. [Defines term]
   - However, there is no agreement as to a 'ranking' of importance for each of the sub factors. Political stability can be interpreted to mean a detailed focus on one sub issue or upon all sub issues. Alternate perspectives must be discussed. This could be established via integration of modernization theory, dependency theory or the Washington Consensus. [Correct focus upon 'Discuss' question stem].
   - A contemporary example of this is Yemen, which has been gripped by civil war (internal conflict) since 2015. Already ranked as the poorest country in the Middle East, 80% of the Yemeni public (24 million people) are now classified by the UN as being in 'great need', 14.3 million of these in 'acute need'. [Link to case study]
   - In 2015 there was a 28% decline in Yemen's GDP, followed by a combined 11% fall between 2016 and 2019. Therefore, political instability, in this case conflict, has had a direct impact upon economic development. In terms of human factors, following 20 years of continual improvement, post 2010, the state's HDI ranking began a slow decline – this decline increased sharply after the start of the conflict in 2015. [Case study focus]

   Discussion points:
   - Full exploration of the critical sub factors relating to political instability, which could be focused upon conflict, ideologies or governance. [Answering question]
   - Analysis of how these sub issues can affect the different measurement indicators related to development is central, as is providing a clear discussion. This could be via consideration of alternative sub issues and evaluating the level of impact, or by providing a balanced counter argument. [Considering the 'Discuss' stem in the question]
   - The statistical data relating to political stability would appear to clearly indicate a negative impact upon development relating to each of the sub focus; however, the true level of impact varies between each. This is most evident at a national level, but regional may also be considered. [Consideration of different levels of analysis]
   - This includes impacts upon key concepts related to globalization, poverty and inequality. [Key concept focus]
   - Case studies may include recent conflicts in South Sudan, Afghanistan or Syria. The recent Boko Haram insurgency and ongoing ideological divisions in Colombia and Egypt are good examples of ideological conflict impacting development. **[25 marks]**

7. Have you remembered and thought about the following in your answer?
   - Peace and conflict is a unit of study that includes different perspectives upon peace, conflict, violence and non-violence.
   - The statement is focused upon violent conflict and the changing nature of violent conflict. [Links to question]
   - Recognition of the changing nature of violent conflict post 1945 (old wars vs. new wars).

- Discussion of the movement away from interstate geo-political, ideologically driven, nation-based conflicts, which are often financed by the state, to intrastate identity-based conflicts, which are funded by seizing control of parts of an economy or criminality. In new wars, the primary participants are now non-state actors. [Defines term]
- A contemporary example of this could be the conflict relating to the Kurds. A complex intrastate conflict spanning several decades and three states (Turkey, Iraq and Syria). [Link to case study]
- Further exploration of the linguistic, cultural, religious and socio-economic basis of the Kurds' usage of violence, primarily against Turkey as the key state actor. [Link to case study]

Discussion points:
- Galtung's model of violent conflict can be expressed at what is termed latent and manifest levels. In the Kurdish conflict, the latent level related to the feelings of disenfranchisement and repression felt by the Kurdish people across the state regimes in which Kurds are spread. This would agree with the statement in question. [Answering question]
- However, there are still visible interstate conflicts which manifest in conflicts over resources or control of territory. A prime example of this is Russia's 2014 annexation of Crimea from Ukraine. [Discussing alternate views to the statement]
- Potential hybrid conflicts also exist, such as Israel's 2006 invasion of Lebanon in which the violent conflict was largely fought against Hezbollah, a non-state actor. This type of state vs. non-state actor conflict is also becoming more prevalent.
- The usage of violence on local, national, regional and other levels is also applicable. [Consideration of different levels of analysis]
- Linkage of case study examples could include the Syrian Civil War from 2015, Iraq 2003–2011, Afghanistan Wars 2001–2014 or the Sudanese Civil War from 2013. **[25 marks]**

8. Have you remembered and thought about the following in your answer?
   - Peace and conflict is a unit of study that includes different perspectives upon peace, conflict, violence and non-violence.
   - The claim is based upon the idea that positive peace, as opposed to negative peace, cannot be attained. Identification of what peace is, largely being defined as the absence of violence or conflict. Peace can also be considered to include not just the absence of violent conflict, but also the existence of a more equitable and just society. [Links to question]
   - Recognition of the differences in the terms positive and negative peace. Negative peace relates to the establishment of truces and ceasefire, meaning the simple absence of violent conflict. On the other hand, positive peace refers to a more fundamental shift in societal behavior in which the systemic causes of the violent conflict can be addressed, leading to a more equitable society. [Defines term]
   - A contemporary example of this could be the civil war in Chad 2005–2010. This violent conflict saw a largely Muslim north pitted against a largely Christian south. Whilst negative peace was established in 2010, there are ongoing attempts to create positive peace by governmental and non-governmental groups, amongst others. [Link to case study]
   - Further exploration of the peace building efforts in Chad pre and post 2010 would provide relevant material. Clan violence, reintegration of militias and projects to build civil society are all focus worthy.

   Discussion points:
   - Two competing perspectives in international relations are visible. Realists advocate that positive peace is not unobtainable. Liberals advocate that positive peace is achievable. [Answering question]
   - Focus could be on establishing a realism anarchic basis in which strength and national security are the primary concerns, negative peace is the best that can be hoped for in such a system, or neo-liberalism's wider approach to achieving equity and forgiveness post conflict. [Examining the statement]
   - Chad has achieved some form of positive peace since 2010, the previous authoritarian President Hissene Habre being sentenced to life imprisonment in Senegal in 2017.
   - The usage of peace-building efforts at local, national, regional and other levels is also applicable. [Consideration of different levels of analysis]
   - Linkage of case study examples could include Colombia's ongoing conflict with FARC rebels or Northern Ireland's Good Friday Agreement (1998) and subsequent power sharing. **[25 marks]**

Set B

Paper 1

1. • Source A depicts a situation in which certain regions are affected by continuing levels of illiteracy e.g. sub-Saharan Africa.
   • Lower literacy rates are visible in sub-Saharan Africa, a region blighted by underdevelopment. Thus, we may draw a correlation between poor educational opportunities and underdevelopment.
   • Higher literacy rates appear linked to areas considered more economically developed, such as Western Europe, North American, Japan and Australia. **[3 marks]**

2. • Source B clearly draws a correlation between a lack of political stability and a lack of foreign direct investment. FDI is often one of the major driving forces behind a state's continued development.
   • Source B therefore also clearly draws a link between limited economic development and a lack of political stability.
   • Source B is published via a blog at the World Bank, displaying a mainstream economic development perspective.
   • Examples studied could include the usage of Somalia as a failed state, thus lacking both FDI and internal economic development. This would be a focus upon conflict as a component of political stability. Additional examples could include both Syria and Libya.
   • In the UK, Brexit and the uncertainty surrounding this, with continuing devaluation of Sterling since the 2016 vote, is also a strong correlation that can be made. This is not a conflict issue affecting political stability, but rather one of governance. **[4 marks]**

3. • Source C is from the UN Committee for Development Policy. It clearly articles a theory of development, which encompasses education, gender and other social factors as issues which limit state development.
   • Source D from the OECD contrasts directly with Source B's outline, establishing the importance of trade liberalization in development, thus placing primacy upon economic factors above all others. This follows a more traditional and mainstream capitalist-based perspective, linked to neo-liberalism.
   • Source D states that free market liberalization has raised the living standards of the lowest 20% of the world's population, practically evidencing via data usage the positive impact an economic development focus can bring.
   • Source C argues that unfettered free markets create greater wealth disparity, which is an ever-increasing global issue.
   • Examples could include focus upon the different models of development measurement, including GINI Index figures displaying growing wealth disparity figures, Happy Planet Index, Inclusive Wealth Index, etc. **[8 marks]**

4. • Answers should establish an understanding of economics as a factor impacting upon state development. Source A and Source B both establish this and can be used as evidence. Links can be drawn with neo-liberal economic theory and prosperity, including Fukayama's 'End of History'.
   • Responses may make note of the competing perspectives apparent from the two IGO organizations, the UN and OECD, which clearly have differing conceptions regarding the primacy of economic factors alone in driving development. This is at the heart of the issues surrounding development theory.
   • However, there are other competing factors including political, social and environmental factors, which also affect development. These could be broken down into appropriate subheadings or dealt with as whole categories.
   • Source B can be used to outline the importance of political instability in inhibiting development; examples could include conflict in Syria, Iraq, Libya and governance via the UK and Brexit.
   • Sources A and C display the importance of social factors in increasing or decreasing development
   • Environmental factors and the impact of trying to develop a sustainable economy can also be articulated. **[10 marks]**

Paper 2

Level/marks breakdown for all Paper 2 answers:
• Level 2 [6–10 marks] show understanding of the question's key concepts
• Level 3 [11–15 marks] discuss counter claims
• Level 4 [16–20 marks] include accurate real-world examples and thoroughly analyse counter claims
• Level 5 [21–25 marks] include case studies and perspectives and evaluate the concepts in a coherent, structured way

1. Have you remembered and thought about the following in your answer?
   • Power, sovereignty and international relations is a unit of study that includes focus upon power, sovereignty, legitimacy and interdependence.
   • Resources often take the form of raw materials (water, food, coal, iron, etc.).
   • However, resources are increasingly becoming linked to the digital economy and the state's digital capacity, not simple raw materials. [Defines term]
   • Power is often measured by a state's control of, or control of others' access to, these resources. [Links to question]
   • However, cultural power, social power and soft power do not take account of these measures. These may be more appropriate as a focus for 21st-century definitions of power. [Correct focus upon 'Evaluate' question stem]
   • A contemporary example of this is the resurgence of Russian influence in global politics. Russia has control of a number of raw material resources necessary for Western Europe to function (oil and natural gas). [Link to case study]
   • Russia's recent digital actions against Georgia, malign intervention in the 2016 US Presidential election and sponsorship of the Fancy Bears hackers would evidence that power is no longer related simply to control of raw materials as resources. [Case study focus]

   Discussion points:
   • Focus upon basic raw materials and links to power – often the greater the access to resources the greater the state's power e.g. China vs. El Salvador. [Answering question]
   • Articulation of different perspectives on power, including realism and neo-realism (Mearshimer), neo-liberalism (Nye) and non-mainstream critical theories (Gramsci), etc., soft power, social power, cultural powers are all valid considerations.
   • Challenges brought to concepts of sovereignty and legitimacy can be explored via the role of NGO and non-state actors in using non-resource-based methods to promote and gain power across inter- or intrastate levels. [Key concept focus and levels of analysis focus]
   • Influence of MNCs and other corporate entities also valid.
   • Recent case studies could include conflict in the South China Sea (2019), ongoing Israeli – Jordanian conflict over water access, or internal conflicts in Congo, Sierra Leone, Liberia or Angola over control of resources. [Case study focus] **[25 marks]**

2. Have you remembered and thought about the following in your answer?
   • Power, sovereignty and international relations is a unit of study that includes focus upon power, sovereignty, legitimacy and interdependence.
   • Intrastate conflict is between two opposing groups internally within a sovereign entity and is often termed civil war. Interstate conflict is between two or more sovereign entities. [Defines term]
   • Intrastate or interstate conflict can both damage and strengthen a state and its sovereignty, dependent upon the outcome of the conflict. [Links to question]
   • A pro- or anti-perspective on the extent of damage caused by both forms of conflict may be taken. [Correct focus upon 'To what extent' question stem]
   • A contemporary example of intrastate conflict damaging the state would be the Syrian civil war which has raged since 2011. Several competing factions have challenged the legitimacy and authority of the Assad regime, with groupings representing government-opposed rebels, the Islamic State and Kurdish militants all vying for control. [Link to case study]
   • External support for the different factions has come from a variety of sources. Russia and Iran have supported the Assad regime with weapons, munitions and direct airstrikes. Turkey has aided the anti-government rebels with the hope of the defeat of the Assad regime, Kurds and IS. These external interventions in an intrastate conflict highlight the damage done to Syria's internal sovereignty and ability to function effectively. [Case study focus]

   Discussion points:
   • Focus upon intrastate conflict vs. interstate conflict. This can include an exposition of the basic functions of a state (law and order, social services, etc.) and the depth of the negative impact of the differing forms of conflict. [Answering question]
   • Often during interstate conflict, the state is able to function effectively until defeat as it is usually its external rather than internal sovereignty that is being challenged (most interstate conflicts are related to territory). The legitimacy of a regime is often enhanced by victory in an interstate conflict, as seen with Putin in Russia during 2014 or Olmert in Israel in 2006.

- This is rarely the case in intrastate conflict, as the domestic basis of the conflict weakens the state's internal sovereignty, with Yemen and Syria being prime examples.
- Challenges brought to concepts of sovereignty and legitimacy can be explored via unilateralism and multilateralism in interstate conflict. [Key concept focus and levels of analysis focus]
- Influence of NATO, UN, African Union and other IGOs in preventing conflict and weakening regimes.
- Recent case studies of intrastate conflicts could include the conflict in Yemen, Syria or South Sudan. Interstate conflict examples could include Israel vs. Lebanon, Russia vs. Ukraine, Coalition vs. Iraq / Coalition vs. Afghanistan. [Case study focus] **[25 marks]**

3. Have you remembered and thought about the following in your answer?
   - Human Rights is a unit of study that includes different perspectives upon human rights, liberty, equality and justice.
   - The key challenges in upholding human rights can be sub-categorized into challenges related to codification, protection, promotion and monitoring. [Links to question]
   - Codification relates to the formalization of rights into law, protection follows codification via judicial structures, promotion includes engagement with civil society to promote human rights and monitoring involves observation of human rights by multiple independent bodies. [Defines term]
   - The primacy given to the exploration of one key challenge versus another would display 'evaluation'. Alternatively, a focus in depth upon an individual challenge at differing levels of analysis (international/regional/national, etc.) would also display evaluative skills, but would limit the focus upon the plural challenges in question stem. [Correct focus on the 'Evaluate' question stem]
   - A contemporary example of this could be by exploring codification issues via the International Convention on Civil and Political Rights, which has been signed by 139 states, establishing international norms. However, certain actors, such as Saudi Arabia, have not signed. This creates a major dichotomy/flaw in international human rights law and practice. [Link to case study]
   - Further exploration of codification as a challenge, in which national level codification is significantly more effective in embedding human rights law. The UK Human Rights Act (2000) or US Bill of Rights (1791) evidences this. [Case study focus]

Discussion points:
- Full exploration of several of the above challenges to upholding human rights. [Answering question]
- Knowledge of a variety of international frameworks for the protection of human rights can be covered including the Universal Declaration of Human Rights (1948), International Convention on Economic Social and Cultural Rights (1966) or International Convention on Civil and Political Rights (1966).
- Focus and evaluation of the United Nations Human Rights Council, UN Office of the High Commissioner for Human Rights, the International Court of Justice and the International Law Commission would all be pertinent.
- Linkage of case study examples could include a focus upon a challenge directly, as outlined above, or via a focus upon an issue/group and the challenge with human rights e.g. political rights in authoritarian states, female rights in patriarchal societies, child labour issues in LEDCs, etc. **[25 marks]**

4. Have you remembered and thought about the following in your answer?
   - Human Rights is a unit of study that includes different perspectives upon human rights, liberty, equality and justice.
   - Knowledge of both human rights and power is required. The relationships between the state's usage of power and delivery of human rights, via practical implementation and a legislative basis. States can be viewed as either the principal violator in human rights atrocities or the essential protector of human rights. [Links to question]
   - Universalism is based upon the universality of rights being applicable to all humans. A state's attempts to implement this may weaken sovereignty by emboldening minority groups or other actors to challenge the state's sovereignty, if groups feel this universalism is lacking. Therefore, the pursuit of universalism in human rights may have either a positive or negative effect upon state power. [Defines term]
   - The stated perspective would correlate with aspects of cultural relativism. It could also be interpreted as relating to authoritarian regimes, in which human rights are often not upheld. Often states with a diffused power basis and strong civil society actors are ones in which human rights are most widely respected and upheld. [Correct focus on the 'Validity' question stem]

- A contemporary example could be the detention in 2019 by the Chinese state of some one million ethnic Uighur and their relocation to educational camps. In a state with a more diffused power basis this would be considered a breach of individual human rights. [Link to case study]
- Actions in Myanmar by the authoritarian regime against the Rohingya would also evidence breaches of basic human rights, in the state's drive to expand its power. [Case study focus]

Discussion points:
- Discussion based upon weakened sovereignty and inability to uphold universal human rights within a state is also central. Discussion may focus around internal and external power. [Answering question]
- The problems related to practical implementation, be they political, economic or cultural rights is also worth consideration.
- However, large strides towards Universalism have been made since 1948s UDHR. Development of further international and national frameworks possible.
- Linkage of case study examples could include focus upon the differences in application of universal human rights in the EU and UK via an accepted judicial mechanism (UK Supreme Court and ECHR) limiting the executive's power and an exploration of issues human rights issues in Israel and the Occupied Palestinian Territories. [Case study focus] **[25 marks]**

5. Have you remembered and thought about the following in your answer?
   - Development is a unit of study that includes different perspectives upon development, globalization, inequality and sustainability.
   - Poverty is an idea that can be defined in differing ways. Extreme poverty is defined by the World Bank as living on under $1.90 per day and in 2016 under 10% of the global population did this.
   - However, wider ideas related to human factors such as access to health care, education and social inclusion can be included in a wider definition and this would put global poverty levels substantially higher. [Defines term]
   - Therefore, poverty as an idea is disputed, and as such, so are both the causes and mechanisms that could be used to alleviate it.
   - Poverty is driven by eight key causes, improper governance being one. Others include a history of colonization, limited education, natural disasters, war and ethnic conflict, overpopulation, lack of employment opportunities and an unequal distribution of wealth. [Links to question]
   - However, theoretical disagreements exist as to where the focus should be placed to tackle the causes. Rostow and modernization theory argue that the focus must be upon eradicating improper governance and establishing stable liberal democratic regimes, which are capitalist and corruption free. Others, such as Frank and Furtado, would argue via dependency theory that having a history of colonization would be of more importance in causing poverty. [Correct focus upon 'Evaluate' question stem]
   - A contemporary example of this would be evident in the exploration of Cote d'Ivore and how, despite significant growth recently in its GDP (from $11 billion in 2001 to $44 billion in 2018, the Cote d'Ivore's CIPA transparency rating (corruption), as measured by the World Bank, has increased sharply at the same time (from a rating of two in 2010 to three in the period 2015–2018). The Cote d'Ivore has increased its HDI index score by approx. 24% since 1990, however, this still places Cote d'Ivore behind other sub-Saharan states such as Ghana, Zambia and Mozambique, showing limited development by comparison to its peers. [Link to case study]
   - Further analysis of Cote d'Ivore would establish large growths in poverty levels between 1988 and 2010 with the proportion of the poor population rising from 10% to 51%. Some decline in this level to 48% in 2018, however, may be due to the reclassification by the World Bank of the extreme poverty levels from $1.20 to $1.90. [Case study focus]

Discussion points:
- Comparison of how development can be limited by improper governance, e.g. Cote d'Ivore vs. Ghana. Evidence of Ghana's positive movement in the HDI Index, improving 31% between 1990 and 2017 and positioning itself at number 149 of 189 states, which correlates with GDP growth from approx. $5 billion in 2001 to $66 billion in 2018, alongside the decline in CIPA transparency rating (corruption), as measured by the World Bank, from three in 2010 to two in 2018. This shows greater development than Cote d'Ivore, with direct correlation to improper governance. [Answering question]

- Articulation of different perspectives on development, including the Structural Adjustment Policies and the Washington Consensus.
- Challenges brought to concepts of inequality and sustainability can be explored by providing focus on alternative causes of poverty and their basis. For example, a focus upon theories of post-colonial economic under-development and exploitation via dependency theory. [Key concept focus and theoretical embedding]
- Discussion of all other causes and their separate or interrelated natures are also valid.
- A recent case study could include measurement towards SDGs on an international or national level, with focus upon one or more of the other seven causes of poverty. [Case study focus]   **[25 marks]**

6. Have you remembered and thought about the following in your answer?
    - Development is a unit of study that includes different perspectives upon development, globalization, inequality and sustainability.
    - Globalization can be defined as the process in which the world is developing into an ever-greater interdependent economic, social and political sphere. This is due to improvements in technology, increasing trade liberalization and a wider movement of people. [Defines term]
    - Globalization has improved transportation and communication, increased states' GNP due to trade liberalization and led to the establishment of enhanced international legal norms. However, wealth inequality is also growing, political polarization is deepening and some theorists view IGOs as limited scope actors. [Links to question]
    - The 'to what extent' question stem allows both agreement and disagreement to be presented, although a judgment must be made. Therefore, both the positive and negative impacts of globalization need to be addressed. [Correct focus upon 'Discuss' question stem]
    - Positive contemporary examples of economic aspects of globalization include the growth of China's GNP increasing from approx. $5 trillion USD in 2009 to $14 trillion USD in 2019. Part of this growth came from a huge increase in Foreign Direct Investment from mid 1990s to 2000s, during serious economic reforms in the country.
    - Globalization as a stimulus is said to have lifted some 700 million Chinese citizens out of poverty, with an increase in GDP per capita from $282 in 1986 to $8100 in 2016. The middle class, in particular, has grown from approx. 4% in 1986 to 31% in 2016.
    - However, China's wealthy inequality is also growing with its GINI coefficient levels rising from 4.6 in 2015 to 4.7 in 2019. [Case study focus]

Discussion points:
- Full exploration of key developments in communications and technology would also be appropriate. Increased multinational corporations' expansions across the developing world has led to higher wage growth, impacting state GDP/GNP also. Negotiations such as the Doha Process have helped with trade liberalization. [Answering question]
- Global governance and the embedding of IGOs and international legal norms are also strong positive arguments.
- Negative aspects to be developed include the misuse of technology and communication advances to sow political instability, such as seen in the US Presidential election in 2016 and Hong Kong protests in 2019. Growing wealth inequality globally, weakening of state sovereignty and negative impacts upon cultural diversity are all also valid arguments.
- Analysis of alternative positives and negatives brought by globalization under the broad umbrella of economic, socio-cultural and political (if related to development). [Considering the 'Discuss' stem in the question]
- Knowledge of all relevant key indicators such as GDP/GNP, GINI Index, HPI and GPI amongst others. [Consideration of different types of development]
- This includes impacts upon key concepts related to globalization, poverty and inequality. [Key concept focus]
- Case studies may include recent development issues in states such as Vietnam, Indonesia or Taiwan.   **[25 marks]**

7. Have you remembered and thought about the following in your answer?
    - Peace and conflict is a unit of study that includes different perspectives upon peace, conflict, violence and non-violence.

- The statement is largely reflective of Webber's theory regarding the state monopoly of violence. [Links to question]
- Arguments surrounding the legitimacy of violence are often characterized via three rationales: religious, moral and self-defence. State usage of violence through warfare or military hard power often depends on one of these three rationales. [Defines term]
- However, there are alternative perspectives, which argue that states alone do not have the monopoly on the legitimate usage of violence. [Correct focus on the 'Discuss' question stem]
- A contemporary example of this could be the Arab Spring of 2011. [Link to case study]
- Further exploration of actions by NATO in Libya, the African Union in Somalia, ISIL in Syria and Iraq could provide the basis for discussion. [Case study focus]

Discussion points:
- Full exploration of the argument, largely related to Webber's theory (1919) that states seek to monopolize the usage of violence. That, indeed, this is necessary for a state to function as part of its legitimization process. [Answering question]
- The role of IGOs in legitimizing violence, the need to be a state to operate within an IGO would precede this.
- Discussion of the 'Just War Doctrine' as a mechanism for establishing legitimacy for violent actions, which in turn raises the balanced, counter arguments. Non-state actors, revolutionary movements and non-violent protests could all be explored. [Considering the other views in the question]
- The usage of violence on local, national, regional and other levels. [Consideration of different levels of analysis]
- Linkage of case study examples could include the Hong Kong protests 2019, Iran Oil Tanker Crisis 2019, Syria 2011 to date and Libya 2011.   **[25 marks]**

8. Have you remembered and thought about the following in your answer?
    - Peace and conflict is a unit of study that includes different perspectives upon peace, conflict, violence and non-violence.
    - The question focuses on concepts related to peace. Knowledge of what armed violence and conflict are can also be displayed, but this should not be the focus for the response. [Links to question]
    - Peacemaking, peacekeeping and peace building each have distinct definitions. Peacemaking can be said to be the prevention of armed conflict between groups via the threat or usage of force by a third actor. Peacekeeping can be said to be continuing a cessation of armed conflict between groups via third party actors willing to use force if required. This can also include usage of neutral observers to oversee the process. Peace building can be described as focusing on rebuilding and reintegrating a state after the end of an armed conflict. This will often focus upon the role of civil society and can include notions related to the building of positive peace. [Defines term]
    - The terms are separate and distinct yet cannot exist in isolation, thus they are interdependent. [Correct focus on the 'Discuss' question stem]
    - A contemporary example of this could be the Haitian civil war, which ended in 2004, and the actions in the state post 2004, which have included peacekeeping and peace building [Link to case study]
    - Further exploration of issues in Lebanon, the Central African Republic or South Sudan could provide the basis for discussion of each of the three key components. [Case study focus]

Discussion points:
- Full exploration of the interrelationship of the three key terms. Ultimately peacekeeping and peace building cannot happen without peacemaking. [Answering question]
- The role of IGOs in all three key components can be explored, specifically the UN or African Union.
- The role of non-state actors, including NGOs such as MSF and the Red Cross, will be relevant to peacekeeping and peace building.
- The cessation of armed conflict on local, national, regional and other levels would be a valid consideration. [Consideration of different levels of analysis]
- Linkage of case study examples could include a detailed focus upon Northern Ireland post 1998, Sudan and South Sudan post 2011 and Yemen 2015 to date.   **[25 marks]**

Set C

Paper 1

1. • Composed of members from all continents
   • Mostly members from Asia and Africa
   • Regions with the fewest members are Eastern Europe and Western Europe.
   Award yourself [1] for each relevant point up to a maximum of [3]. Other relevant points not listed can also be rewarded. **[3 marks]**

2. • The HRC encourages states to protect rights
     – by encouraging them to complete periodic reviews that are reliant on state co-operation.
   • The HRC has a monitoring process to check on Human Rights abuses
     – meaning states are encouraged to complete their pledges.
   • Examples could include states that have accepted periodic review and acted upon this information, such as Uganda, whose review in 2014 led to the completion of its pledge to introduce an independent human rights-monitoring commission.

   You don't need to make four different points for this question. Each correct point will gain you [2] marks to a total of [4]. To be awarded [2] a point must be well developed; for example, simply making the point that the HRC can protect human rights would be awarded [1], whereas developing this point into a comment such as 'the HRC can encourage states to protect citizens rights by encouraging states to participate in periodic reviews that are reliant on state co-operation' would be awarded [2].

   You can get a maximum of [3] without referencing an example studied. **[4 marks]**

3. Responses could include the following points of comparison/contrast
   • States may challenge the protection of human rights if it is not in their interest to adhere to universal human rights laws.
   • Both the USA and ASEAN nations are broadly in favour of human rights.
   • Protection of human rights may be difficult as states are not able to control what happens beyond their border.
   • Human rights may be of less importance than geopolitical concerns.
   • States may act on identifying human rights abuses but as a result of an inability to act or an ideological unwillingness they may not uphold human rights.
   • With human rights there are issues of sovereignty; states will be unwilling to allow IGO monitoring.

Source C	Source D
Human rights abuses were permitted by the US to their allies if it was in the interest of the US.	Voluntary participation in periodic review among ASEAN countries is universal.
Human rights were used by politicians to push political aims rather than being a genuine commitment to improving lives.	ASEAN states are not open minded to international monitoring procedures.
The problems with different ideological perspectives on human rights makes their enforcement difficult.	There is no human rights protection system in any of the ASEAN states.
	Although they are signatories to international treaties, national governments are not following these rules.

Discussing the view of only one source is worth a maximum of [4]. If two sources are discussed separately with no linking between them, your maximum is [4]. If you focused mostly on one source with only minimal reference to the other source, your maximum is [5]. You gain [2] marks per effective point of contrast, up to a maximum of [8]. An [8] response answer should present a detailed running contrast and can contain answers different from those above. **[8 marks]**

4. Question 4 is assessed according to the generic IB mark bands, in conjunction with these marking notes.
   Source material may include, but is not limited to:

Source A:
   • The greatest concentration of political power rests with African and Asian states who may use this to dominate the HRC.
   • The composition of the HRC is not even and therefore may lead to issues of states overstating their power and using human rights as a political tool.

Source B:
   • The HRC is limited in its power as it relies on state compliance. As a result, this may lead to states choosing to ignore human rights so they are not politicized.
   • As the HRC has established clear protocols these could be used to politicize the issue of human rights.
   • The monitoring protocol can be used by states in order to use human rights as a foreign policy tool.

Source C:
   • The US during the Cold War used human rights and human rights activism as a political tool.
   • US politicization of rights was a choice in order to advance foreign policy goals.
   • The US may not have genuinely cared about rights, given its failure to address abuses conducted by its allies.
   • Politicians 'strategically deployed' human rights.

Source D:
   • The process of human rights reporting leaves governments open to challenge.
   • All ASEAN countries have agreed to periodic review but still abuse rights, which may show they have done this as a political tool.
   • 'Comprehensive human rights protection is absent in every country' shows that no amount of political pressure will protect rights.

Own knowledge may include, but is not limited to:
Arguments that politicization hampers the application of human rights:
   • States use human rights as an excuse to fulfil wider geopolitical aims.
   • States may act in politically charged ways that hinder the universal application of human rights.
   • States may feel a western version of rights has been imposed rather than there being a truly universal set of rights, which leads to perceived political bias and exclusion from the human rights regime.

Arguments that politicization of human rights does not endanger the application of rights:
   • As human rights are assumed as universal they cannot be used as a political tool as it is merely encouraging all states to follow an agreed set of norms.
   • Politicization of rights allows greater discussion of how rights should and should not be applied, which ultimately serves to protect rights of vulnerable people.

You might have made other valid points or examples. You won't have time to make as many points in your answer as the example points listed.
You should use evidence from the sources **and** your own knowledge of key concepts **and** from your own study. If you have **only** used source material **or** own knowledge then you can get a maximum of [6] marks.
To achieve all [10] marks, you must refer to all four sources. **[10 marks]**

Paper 2

> **Level/marks breakdown for all Paper 2 answers:**
> • Level 2 [6–10 marks] show understanding of the question's key concepts
> • Level 3 [11–15 marks] discuss counter claims
> • Level 4 [16–20 marks] include accurate real-world examples and thoroughly analyse counter claims
> • Level 5 [21–25 marks] include case studies and perspectives and evaluate the concepts in a coherent, structured way

1. Have you remembered and thought about the following in your answer?
   • Your answer should show a clear understanding of the concepts of NGOs, MNCs and trade unions. You should show an awareness of the work of these different bodies.
   • NGOs can be organizations that work outside the sphere of national governments in a range of functions. Organizations could include: the Red Cross, Amnesty International, Greenpeace, and many more.

- MNCs are to be understood as corporations with assets in more than one country. Examples include: Amazon, Nike, Unilever, and many more.
- Trade unions are organizations that advocate for workers' rights. An example is the International Trade Union Confederation (ITUC).

Each of these actors has an impact in multiple ways. In order to judge their impact, you need to reference some of the key concepts in unit 1: Power, sovereignty, legitimacy and interdependence. You should show that each of these actors may have a different agenda, motive, strategy and impact, and distinguish between them.
Reasons why NGOs, MNCs and trade unions may have an impact on global politics include:

- These actors benefit from the globalization that enables them to have an impact across borders. Examples of this may include the work of MSF in West Africa's Ebola crisis, where they were able to operate outside the bounds of the states.
- Non-state actors have a wide reach. They have broad support globally, which can give them the advantage of leverage over states. An example of this could be ITUC, which has over 200-million members in over 160 countries worldwide.
- The financial power of MNCs can be significant in how they are able to operate. The revenue of some MNCs may exceed the GDP of small states, giving them significant economic power. Examples may include the tax arrangements for MNCs, such as Amazon and the failure of Nike to adhere to labor laws in Honduras.
- Trade unions' collective bargaining power can aid individual workers in defending their rights against governments. Examples of this could include the general workers' strike in India in response to the allegedly anti-worker policies of the BJP.
- Non-state actors may be able to work more effectively in areas where conflict or disaster has led to fragile or failed states. Examples of this could be the work of the Red Crescent in Yemen.
- NGOs have an advantage of specializing in particular areas. This may give them greater expertise and knowledge of how to resolve issues. Examples of this could include the work of HRW in documenting and alerting IGOs and states to abuses of human rights.

Arguments why NGOs, MNCs and trade unions do not necessarily have an impact on global politics could include:

- From a realist world view, states may be considered as the highest actor. They can use hard power to stop NGOs and defend their sovereignty. An example of this could be the expulsion of MSF workers by Sudan.
- Some organizations may be limited by budgets and are reliant on donations from the public. This could leave them with less power.
- Trade unions in many states have seen their power eroded in recent years, with strikes broken and governments able to dictate terms in negotiations. An example of this could be the failure of the Federation of Trade Unions in Hong Kong to negotiate on working hours and pay.
- Some MNCs and NGOs may face accusations of a deficit in legitimacy that may affect their support and ability to act.

You should include specific examples in your answer but they don't have to be the examples above. You could cite cases of states having greater power than non-state actors. You may choose to focus on the issue of sovereignty and the challenges that NGOs, MNCs and trade unions pose to the sovereignty of a state. Alternatively, you could look at power as the defining measure of impact.

Good answers will also reference that interdependence is essential for many of these actors to act effectively. You could conclude by discussing how you think NGOs, MNCs and trade unions are having an impact on global politics today. **[25 marks]**

2. Have you remembered and thought about the following in your answer? You should show that you understand the concept of power as, defined in the guide, the ability to effect change. You should also be able to define the difference between hard power (using military means and economic sanctions to force change) and soft power (using persuasion and influence to effect change). You should also support your points with suitable case study examples. For top marks you might evaluate that a combination of the two types of power (smart power) is more effective and may also discuss the rise of sharp power in recent years.
Reasons soft power is only effective if combined with hard power may include:

- Soft power can be limited in its effectiveness if the state concerned can resist through hard power. Examples of this could

be the presence of Confucius institutes in the USA: their effect has been limited whereas the economic power in the recent trade war could be argued to have had a greater effect on the relationship between the states.
- In cases of confrontation, soft power will not help a state to defend sovereignty if the other state or actor is not influenced by this.
- More powerful states may be able to exert soft power; however, the ability to influence is less effective for smaller states. Examples could reference the USA's cultural reach in comparison to that of smaller states.
- Hard power can pave the way for the conditions that allow soft power to spread. Examples may be how states have used coercion followed by campaigns to influence, such as China with its aid and propaganda campaign in the Tibetan autonomous region.
- State building or regime change may be reliant on hard power to initiate change with soft power deployed once change has been made in order to embed the regime. Examples of this may discuss Iraq post 2003.

Arguments that soft power can be effective without the need for hard power may include:

- Regime change through use of hard power only can lead to disintegration in a new state if the people have not been persuaded of the benefits of the change. Examples to support this point may include the difficulties of regime change in Afghanistan, Iraq and Libya.
- Soft power can achieve geopolitical gains without the need for deployment of hard power. Examples of this may reference the growing strategic alliances developed by China through the One Belt One Road policy.
- Soft power can achieve lasting outcomes that enable states to influence one another for longer periods whereas hard power may only allow temporary shifts in power that without embedding can be lost.
- Soft power can be a tool that allows alliances to develop and prevents the need for the use of hard power to bring change. This could be seen in the development of the Western liberal rules-based order influenced by the United States.

In your answer you should be aware of the nuances of the quote: that soft power is not considered irrelevant; however, it can only function effectively if a state has the hard power tools to effect change. If you bring in the idea of smart and sharp power to develop the argument further, then this would show considering other perspectives. You should support theoretical arguments with specific contemporary examples. **[25 marks]**

3. Have you remembered and thought about the following in your answer? Human rights have been developed over time through a range of actors in global politics, from local customs through to states who have included rights as part of their constitutions, and intergovernmental organizations that have passed treaties to codify the fundamental human rights outlined in the declaration of human rights.
You should demonstrate a clear understanding of human rights and that human rights may be used by states to enhance their power. You should reference the challenge human rights laws and treaties may pose to the sovereignty of states (e.g. the difficulty that may be created when intergovernmental laws conflict with laws at a state level). You should also reference specific human rights laws and treaties such as the ICCPR and ICESCR.
Arguments that the impact of treaties and laws has enhanced the ability of states to protect human rights:

- States can define their own conception of human rights, which enhances their ability to protect human rights without costing their sovereignty. For example, South Africa developed its constitution with human rights incorporated in order to overcome historical issues.
- States as signatories to the ICCPR and ICESCR have an international legal framework to guide them on how to act to protect human rights. For example, Australia overturned a law preventing gay marriage after consultation with the ICESCR.
- States that are unable to prosecute abusers of human rights have the Rome Statute and the ICC to help. For example, the DR Congo had the trial of warlord Thomas Lubanga held in the ICC.
- The creation of treaties that are more relevant to the context that states operate in may enhance their ability to protect human rights. For example, the Banjul Charter helps African states to defend collective rights.
- In signing these treaties and laws, states are not always sacrificing their sovereignty as most are voluntary agreements

and states choose to participate in them. For example, Canada initially refused to sign the UNDRIP as it was incompatible with its constitution.

Arguments that the impact of treaties and laws has not enhanced the ability of states to protect human rights:
- By signing some treaties and laws, states may be sacrificing a part of their sovereignty. For example, the UK battle with the European Court of Human Rights around the voting rights of prisoners.
- Human rights treaties may be overly politicized and used to single out states unfairly, leading to some members pulling out and therefore limiting their ability to protect rights. For example, the threat of withdrawal by Burundi from the ICC.
- Although many treaties are codified, they lack power, relying on states to enforce them, which leaves them open to abuse. For example, Russia's laws on anti-homosexual propaganda breach the ICCPR but are encouraged by the state.

Your answer must include some specific references to individual treaties and laws in order to access the top bands. These treaties may include: ICCPR, ICESCR, UNDRIP, Banjul Charter, Rome Statute, ECHR.

You answer should be clear on whether you think the protection of human rights is ultimately the responsibility of the state or another supranational actor. To access more than 10 marks (Level 3) you also need to examine counter claims. **[25 marks]**

4. Have you remembered and thought about the following in your answer? Responses should demonstrate an understanding of the key concepts in the question, that of interdependence being the mutual reliance between states and other groups. In this case non-state actors may refer to IGOs concerned with human rights such as the UNHCR or NGOs such as Amnesty International. Good answers may bring in the related concepts of globalization as a force for increasing levels of interdependence alongside changing power relationships and the impact on sovereignty as interdependence increases. The effectiveness of human rights laws and treaties should be discussed with an emphasis on whether greater interdependence leads to more effective prosecution of human rights abuses.

Arguments that human rights laws become more effective as a result of greater interdependence between states and non-state actors may include:
- That human rights are a transnational issue and require a transnational approach to their creation, monitoring and enforcement, implicitly this requires greater involvement by a range of actors.
- With increased interdependence between states there may be a willingness to share responsibility for enforcement of laws and treaties to which they agree regardless of the states' self-interest, which may make human rights laws more effective.
- States are able to share the responsibility to enforce these laws and treaties, this means that regardless of cost or other impediments weaker states may be able to rely on stronger states to help enforce human rights laws.
- The creation of international institutions that foster interdependence such as the UN Human Rights Council and International Criminal Court is necessary for human rights laws and treaties to be effective, these institutions have a mandate (and in the case of the ICC, power) to effectively enforce human rights laws.
- The role of NGOs such as Amnesty and Human Rights Watch help to raise awareness of where human rights laws have been challenged. Cooperation and pressure on states by NGOs enhances the effectiveness of human rights laws.

Arguments that human rights laws are **not** more effective if there is greater interdependence between states and non-state actors may include:
- The role of NGOs can often be ignored by states and therefore the pressure that may be exerted by campaigns such as Amnesty's 'write for rights' is limited if states are not open to enforcing human rights laws.
- Interdependence between states is not always necessary as some human rights are embedded into national constitutions and/or bills of rights, and therefore states can unilaterally defend human rights.
- Interdependence between states may have created covenants and treaties that defend human rights, however, these are voluntary and states can choose not to participate or withdraw (such as South Africa and the ICC).

- States may well place greater importance on their own sovereignty rather than risk their power in defending human rights laws in another state.
- Accusations that many non-state actors such as Amnesty or the ICC have an inherent bias against certain regions may limit the effectiveness of interdependence in defending human rights laws.

Responses should make clear reference to instances where states and non-state actors have worked closely to enforce human rights laws. Good answers may distinguish between different groups of non-state actors.
Responses should clearly evaluate whether interdependence is the most important consideration when ensuring the effectiveness of human rights laws. This judgement should be reached by discussing relevant contemporary examples of where human rights laws have and have not been effective. **[25 marks]**

5. Have you remembered and thought about the following in your answer? Development as a concept should be considered as the sustained increase in the standard of living and well-being. This increase in the standard of living could be measured or seen through a variety of factors including (but not limited to) economic growth, reduced inequality, reduced poverty and sustainable production.

You should demonstrate a clear understanding of the given factor, environment and sustainability. Sustainability as a concept is defined as development that meets the needs of the present without compromising the ability of future generations to meet their needs. Development considering this factor could then be compared to a range of other factors, including political factors, economic factors, social factors and institutional factors. Responses should support all points with specific examples of where development has occurred as a result of a factor being enacted.

Arguments that environment and sustainability are more critical considerations for development than economic and political factors include:
- Sustainable methods to achieve development can achieve long-term economic benefits. Examples could reference development of education programmes, such as the sustainable education project in Singapore.
- Environmental factors such as resource endowment may help enable states to provide citizens with institutions that aid development. Examples could reference the development of living standards in Dubai as a result of oil wealth.
- Environmental considerations are often directly linked to measures of development and well-being, such as health and well-being. Examples of environmental development could focus on the growth of renewable energy in China to alleviate air pollution or the great green wall in sub-Saharan Africa.
- The notion that sustainable development is crucial for large swathes of the population. The focus could be on the importance of alleviating inequality between genders. Examples of work in this area could include the growth in representation of women in Rwanda's government.
- Sustainable and environmental development can encourage new industries and develop economic growth. Examples could include the development of new technologies such as wireless charging electric buses in Bristol, UK.

Arguments that economic and political factors may be more critical considerations for development than those linked to sustainability and environment factors could include:
- Long-term development may be impossible if there is a history of persistent conflict and violence preventing the development of institutions aiding development. Political problems need to be resolved before there can be any effective exploitation of environmental resources. Examples could reference issues in states with a persistent history of conflict, such as the Democratic Republic of Congo.
- Political culture is important in building a culture of equality, which in turn may lead to sustainable development. Examples may reference the development of laws and institutions in states such as South Africa to foster a culture of equality.
- Economic factors may be more significant in states that have a high level of debt and therefore cannot afford to build potentially costly sustainable projects.
- Access to resources is important for any state looking to increase the standard of living of its citizens. States that struggle with access to critical resources may find their development affected by this issue more than considerations of sustainability.

Your answer should make clear reference to instances where states and non-state actors have used different methods to develop. Good answers may conclude that combinations of factors can be more powerful and that focusing on just political or sustainable factors in isolation will not lead to a sustained increase in well-being.

Your answer should clearly evaluate whether sustainability is the most important consideration when considering development. You may choose to look at one or more other factors when reaching a judgement. This judgement should be reached by discussing relevant contemporary examples of where policies to develop states have and have not been effective. **[25 marks]**

6. Have you remembered and thought about the following in your answer? Your answer should demonstrate a clear understanding of intergovernmental organizations (IGOs) and development. Development is defined as the sustained increase in the standard of living and well-being. Your answer might argue that IGOs may be limited in their effectiveness as they are reliant on states supporting their work. The efforts of IGOs may be small relative to those of big corporations and governments. It may also mention that some of the development projects of IGOs are focused on addressing and promoting future developments and the long-term nature of some of their goals may lead some to concluding that IGOs are ineffective.

Arguments in favour of the claim that IGOs have a limited effect on development may include:
- IGOs may focus on broad development objectives rather than more narrow and immediate aspects of development. This could lead to a failure to enact tangible change.
- Development depends on so many factors (economic, social, political) that IGOs are unable to stimulate development alone.
- Governments of Less Economically Developed Countries (LEDCs) may become dependent on assistance from IGOs (e.g. Afghanistan, Chad).
- IGOs with a wide remit may provide aid that is inappropriate or not needed.
- IGOs are reliant on the co-operation of states to allow them to operate. This brings in aspects of sovereignty and fears that states may have over losing this to IGOs.
- IGOs can be manipulated by more powerful state governments. IGOs operate only with the permission of governments, and these can revoke access if they do not like the actions of the IGOs.
- IGOs may be dominated by more powerful states that may use their influence to focus on certain development objectives or political aims. You could reference the Washington Consensus, despite its historical nature.

Arguments against the claim that IGOs have a limited effect on development may include:
- IGOs are effective as a result of historical experience handling development issues, which may make them more effective than NGOs and states. For example, UN refugee agencies such as UNRWA have over 70 years of experience working in Palestine.
- IGOs can access large funds, which enable them to act when NGOs may be more concerned with fundraising. For example, UNICEF had over $5 billion USD in funding last year compared with the Smile foundation and Save the Children, which combined had a budget of less than $3 billion USD.
- The involvement of states in IGOs may give them more power to act and help to resolve issues of development. For example, the ASEAN Human Development Organisation has been founded with a mandate from ten countries to improve workplace conditions.
- The scale of many IGOs means that they can have an influence beyond the states that they serve. For example, the African Development Bank Group has 80 member states comprising both 54 regional countries and 26 non-regional countries.

Your answer should contain references to specific examples. For example, the African Development Bank group and UNICEF have played a large role in improving sanitation and tackling the HIV/AIDS epidemic in Africa.
Your answer may include discussion of how IGOs have historically aided development and the continued work they do in comparison to the small-scale projects of some NGOs.
Responses should include a discussion of whether intergovernmental organizations (NGOs) have a limited effect on development. **[25 marks]**

7. Have you remembered and thought about the following in your answer? Your answer should demonstrate an understanding of the key concept of conflict. Conflict can be defined as the dynamic process of actual or perceived opposition between individuals and groups.

This question looks at the ideas of parties to conflict; your answer should examine the statement, considering the responsibility of states, intrastate groups, protest groups and individuals in causing conflict. Your answer might argue that although one party could be considered largely responsible for conflict, the dynamic nature of conflict means that individuals or groups may also contribute at different periods.

Arguments that states are largely responsible for conflict may include:
- Discussion of the level of conflict: interstate conflict may be mostly the responsibility of states clamouring for power or control of a region. An example is the South China Sea dispute between China and Vietnam around the Paracel islands.
- Points on the causes of conflict that may intersect with the aims of states; for example, territorial control may naturally mean that conflict emerges between states. For example, India and Pakistan's clash over Kashmir.
- The idea that states have the power to easily induce other parties to conflict, including individuals who can be controlled, and therefore they are the only actors truly responsible for conflict.
- Examples of recent conflicts, such as that between Russia and Ukraine where territory and resource disputes led to a development of conflict between states.
- Examples where there are global disputes that are not the responsibility of intrastate groups, such as the dispute between Iran and the USA over the production of nuclear materials.

Arguments that states are not solely responsible for conflict may include:
- Conflicts at state level are less common than conflict between intrastate groups. Examples may include reference to the violence in the Philippine region of Mindanao between the state and Islamic extremists.
- Individual conflict can be far more common at local or community level and result in more significant conflicts emerging over time.
- Interdependence between states is usually a significant incentive to avoid conflict, and as such states are not usually responsible for conflict as they would prefer peace in order to develop. Examples could be given of the development of the European Community.
- Arguments based around the idea that states in a liberal world may be competing in non-violent ways, which may lead to mutually beneficial outcomes if they avoid conflict.
- States often resort to negotiation rather than conflict, whereas protest groups use conflict and confrontation as a tactic to try to increase the power of their demands. For example, the anti-extradition protest movement in Hong Kong.

Your answer should make clear reference to instances where states and non-state actors have experienced conflict. Good answers may introduce a perspective that while states are responsible for conflict, they may be reacting to the actions of non-state actors.

Your answer should clearly evaluate if states are more responsible for the development of conflict. This judgement should be reached by discussing relevant contemporary examples of where conflicts have emerged. **[25 marks]**

8. Have you remembered and thought about the following in your answer? Your answer should show that you understand the key concept of peace. Peace can be defined as the absence of conflict, to a state of harmonious relations. With any definition of peace, you should examine the difference between the ideas of positive and negative peace in relation to the question. You will also need to show an understanding of the theory of structural violence, a concept wherein the structures of the state or a state institution may cause harm. In considering this question, you should look at the different ideas of peacemaking, peacekeeping and peace building, to assess the impact of structural violence on each stage. You might argue that at the stage of negative peace, structural violence may occur; however, as a conflict moves towards positive peace the need to tackle structural violence becomes greater.

Arguments that peace is impossible when there is structural violence may include:
- That structural violence prevents the conditions for positive peace forming, which will hinder any efforts at creating a lasting state of harmonious relations. Examples of this could be conflicts where negative peace has been achieved but underlying conflict remains, such as in the Niger delta.
- There is a link between the presence of structural violence and development. If structural violence is present then there may still be issues with human development, such as gender discrimination,

which if present, would make a lasting peace impossible. Examples of this could include the #metoo movement in the USA.

- Because peace is a dynamic process, if the conditions of structural violence remain then a conflict could re-emerge as the original conditions that triggered violence have not been resolved. This could be seen in the resurgence of violence in Afghanistan.
- A negative peace does not solve the issues of welfare for the people in a state; a failure to tackle these issues may lead to an escalation in conflict and potentially violence. An example is the recent Gillet Jaunes riots in France.

Arguments that peace is possible even when there is structural violence may include:

- Because peace can be both negative and positive, you could argue that peace is possible as there is an absence of violence in many conflicts even when harmonious relations between the state and citizens have not been achieved. The situation in Mindanao in the Philippines is an example of this.
- Recognizing structural violence is often difficult, which makes it more difficult to end. Therefore it may be considered unrealistic to aspire to a situation where there are no conditions of institutional violence.
- Some states may be considered peaceful, even if a small group may suffer structural violence. An example of this could be discrimination against sex workers in Sweden preventing them from accessing government support.
- International efforts to create peace generally focus on peacemaking and peacekeeping. Therefore, this could be considered as peace even if there are still issues with peace building and structural violence. Examples of such action could be the UN-led mission in Cote D'Ivoire.

Your answer should contain references to specific examples. You might focus on examples of negative peace to show that the absence of conflict is possible even if structural violence persists. Good answers may also consider more developed states, which would be considered peaceful, but still have some issues of structural violence. You may evaluate that lasting peace, which avoids direct violence is possible with structural violence; however, in these cases states may still fall into conflict. **[25 marks]**

NOTES

NOTES